My name is

....

My learning goals and success criteria:

- I can trace and write all lower-case letters of the alphabet in NSW Foundation style.
- I can trace and write all capital letters of the alphabet in NSW Foundation style.
- I can trace and write the numerals 1 to 10 in NSW Foundation style.

Are you ready to write?

Posture

Is your back resting against the chair?

Are your feet flat on the floor?

Paper position

left-handed

Are you holding the paper steady with your non-writing hand?

right-handed

Pencil grip

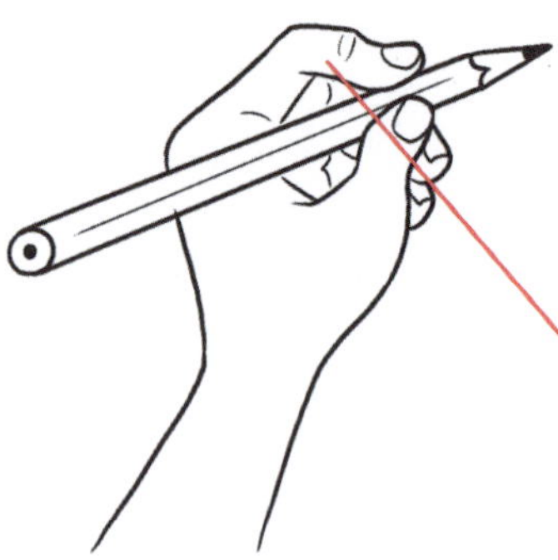

Is one finger on top of the pencil?

Left-handers, hold your pencil a little further up so you can see your handwriting!

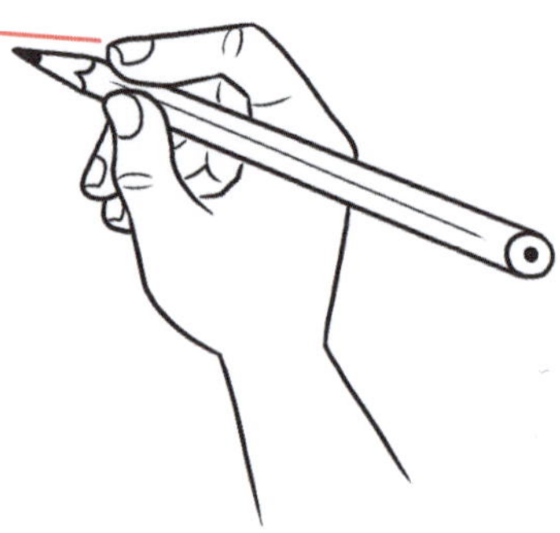

1, 2, 3, 4! Are my feet flat on the foor?
5, 6, 7, 8! Is my back up nice and straight?
9, 10, 11, 12! Show me how your pencil's held!
Thumb and pointer side-by-side, lucky tall one takes a ride!

Start at the red dots. Follow the arrows.

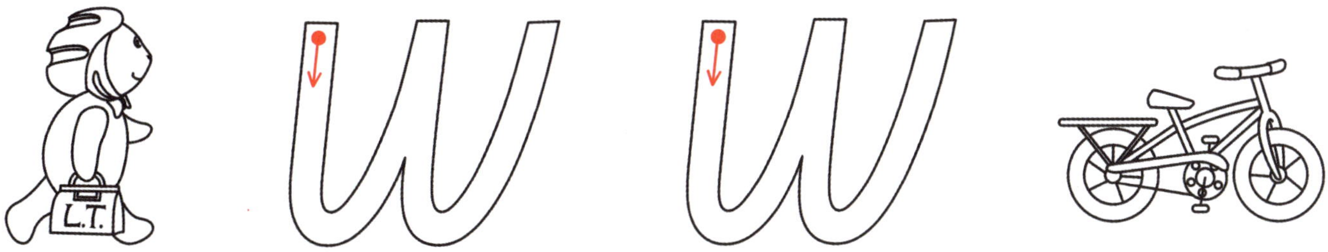

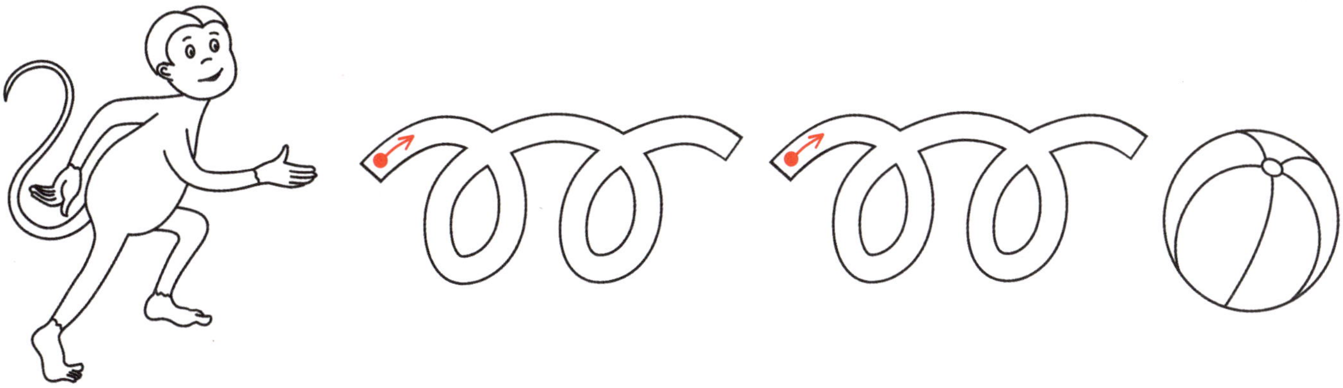

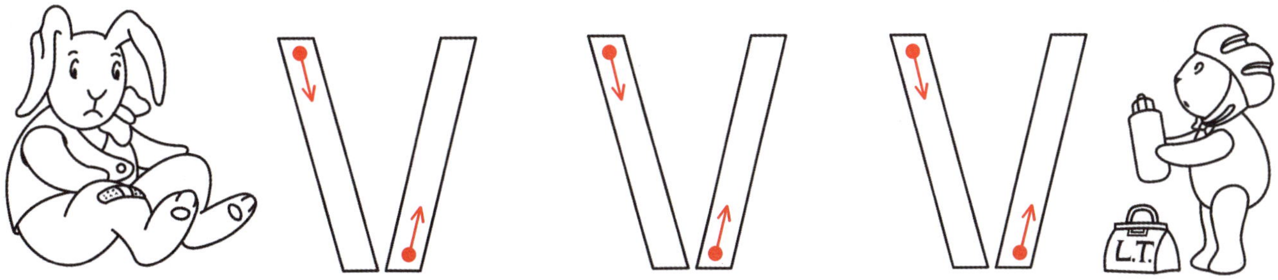

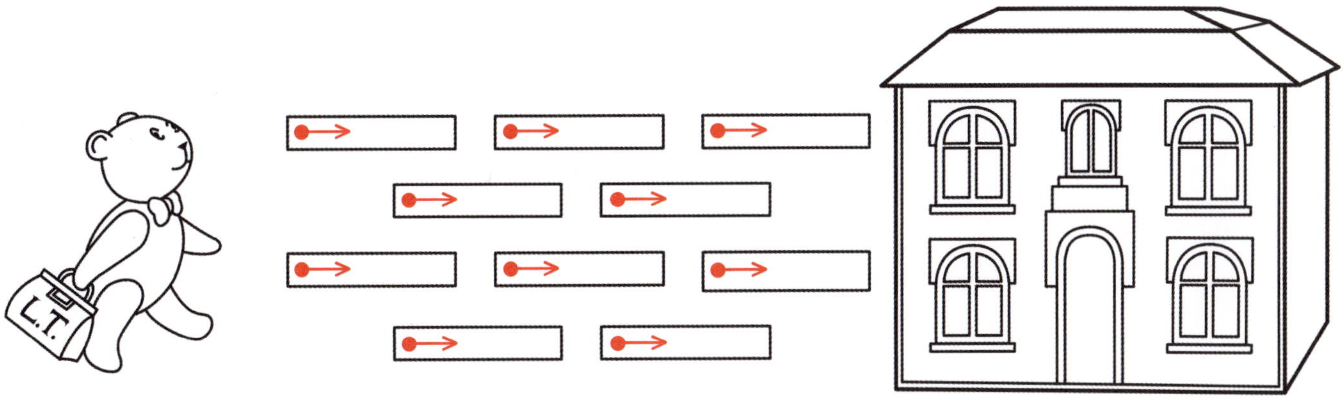

Start at the red dots. Follow the arrows.

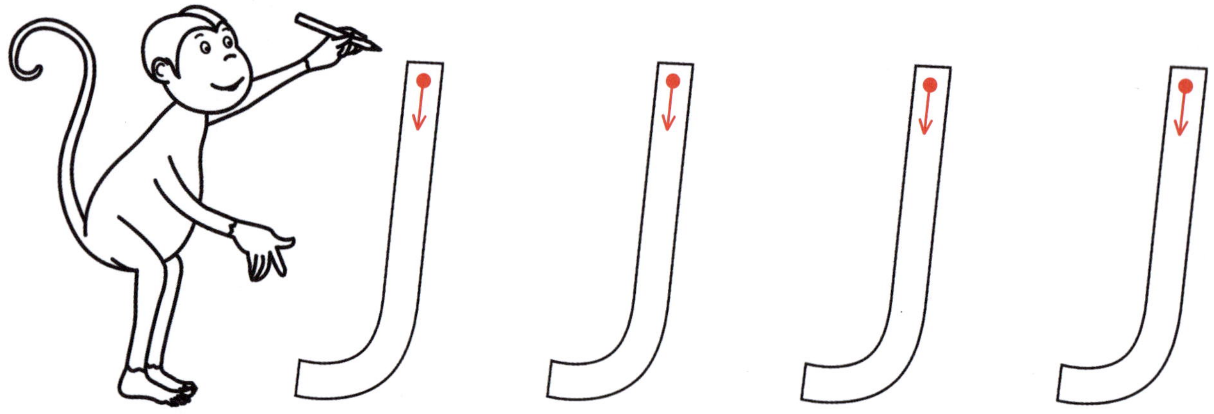

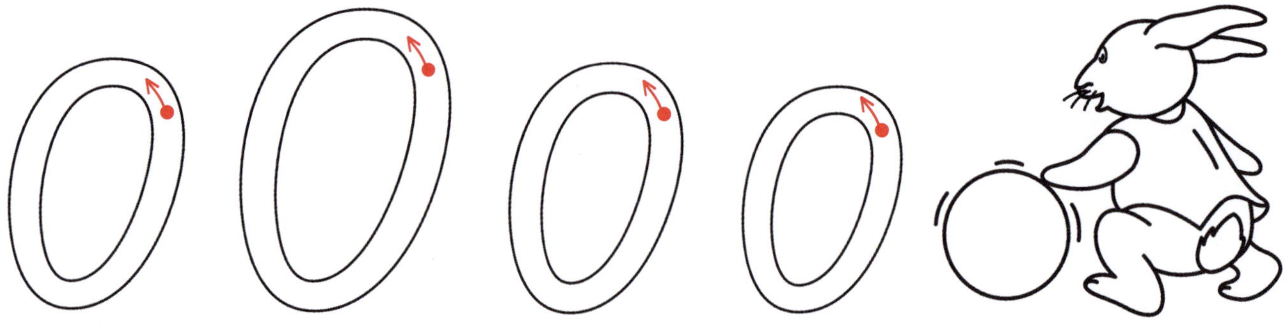

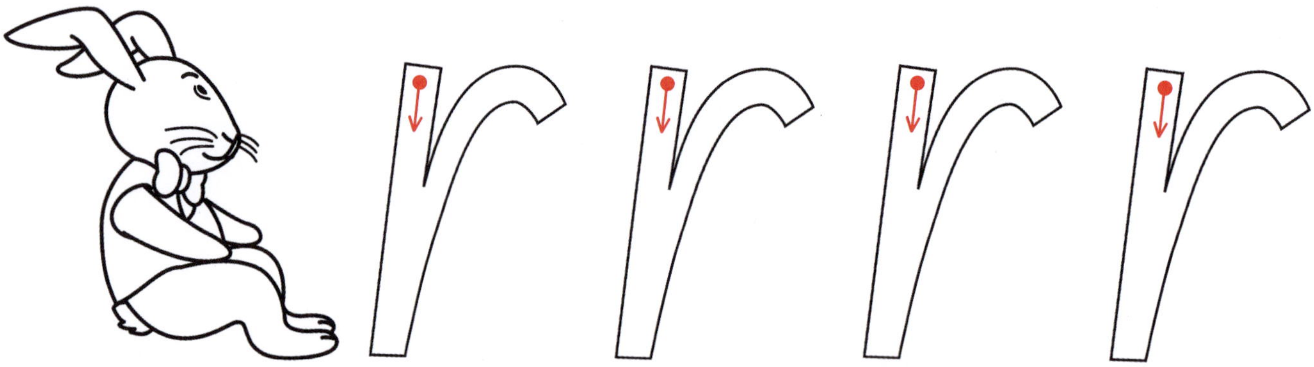

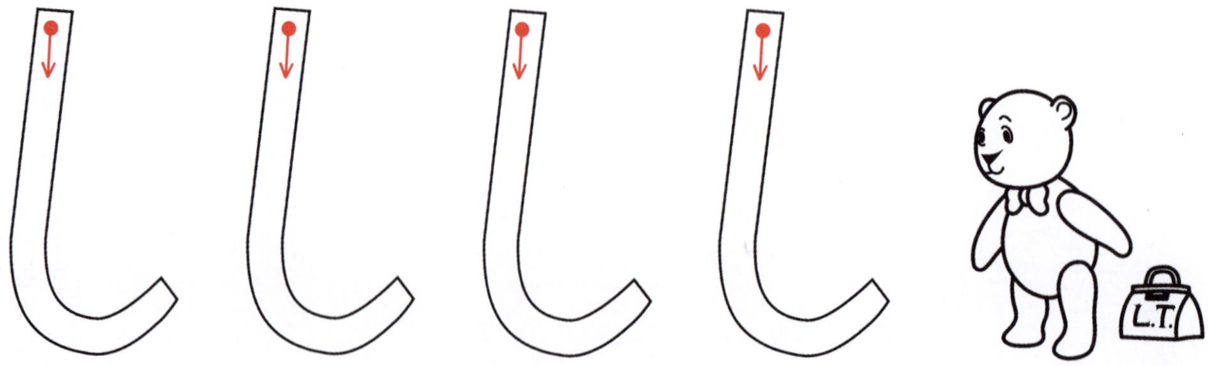

Start at the red dots. Follow the arrows.

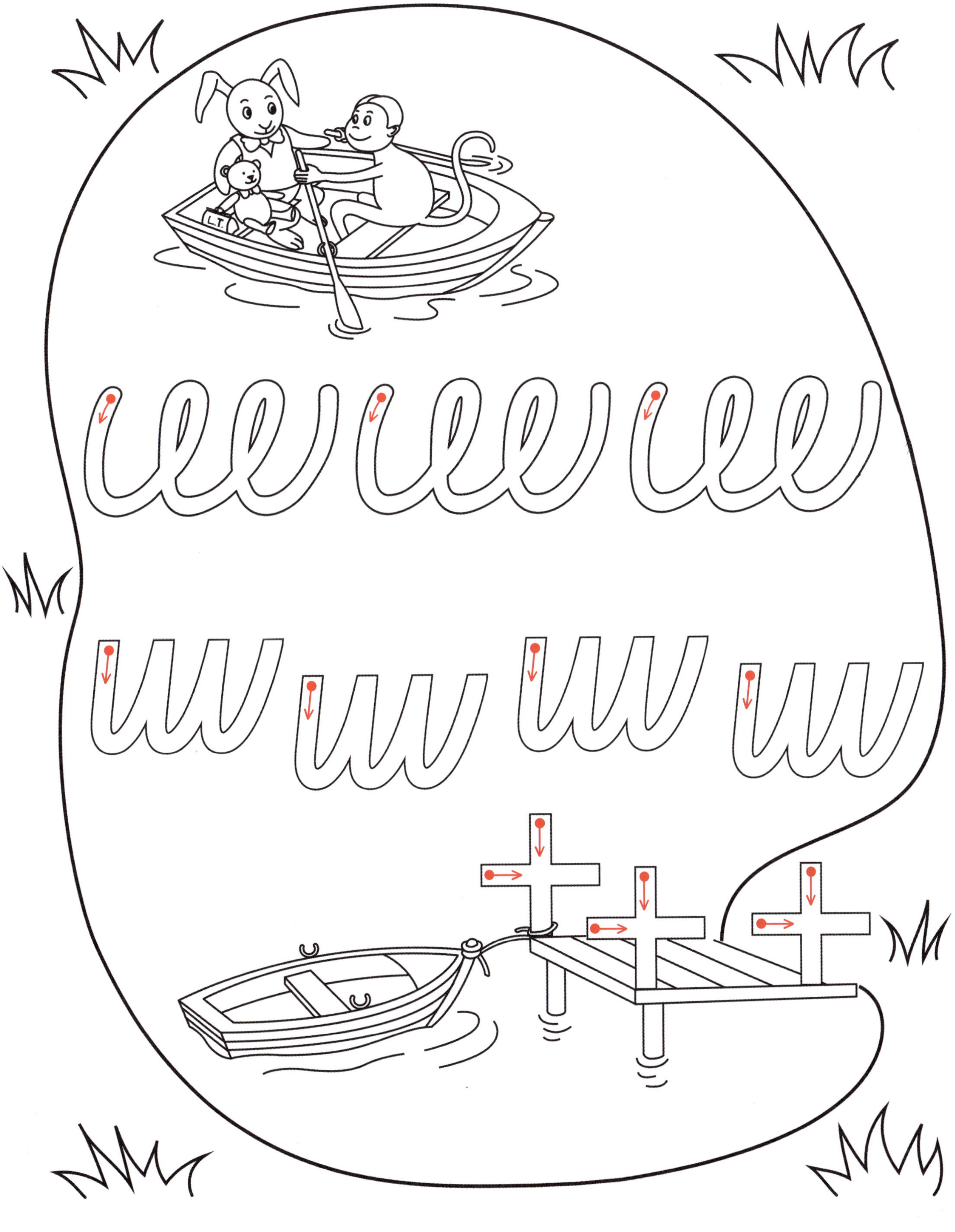

Start at the red dots. Follow the arrows.

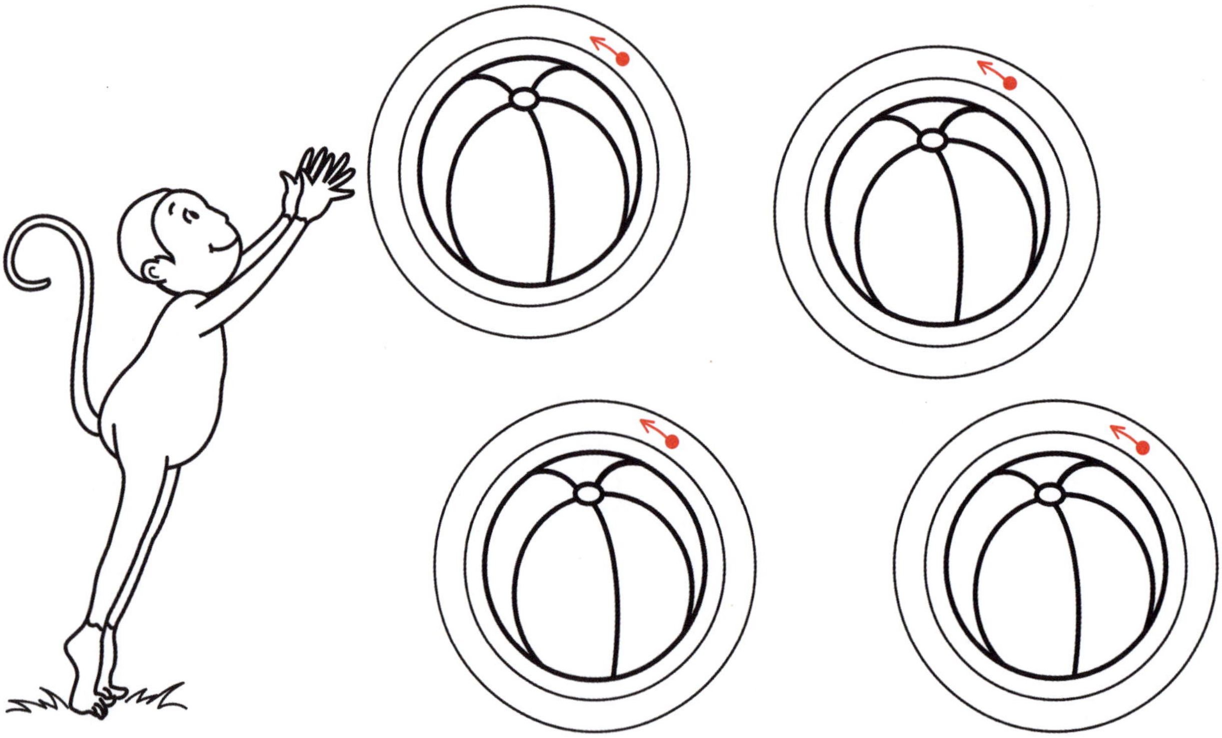

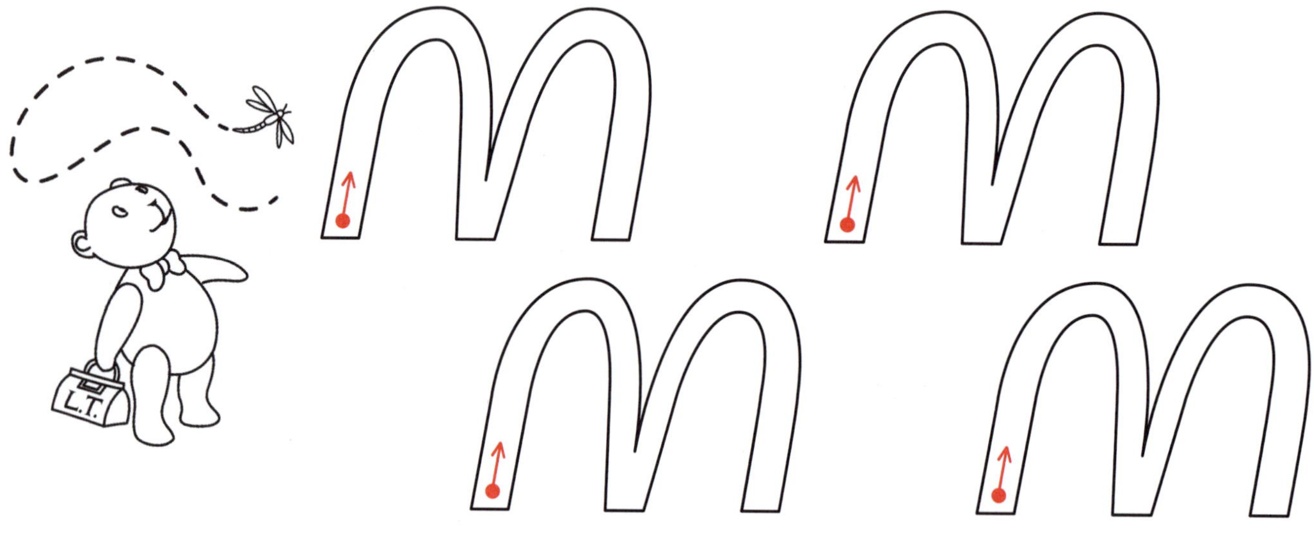

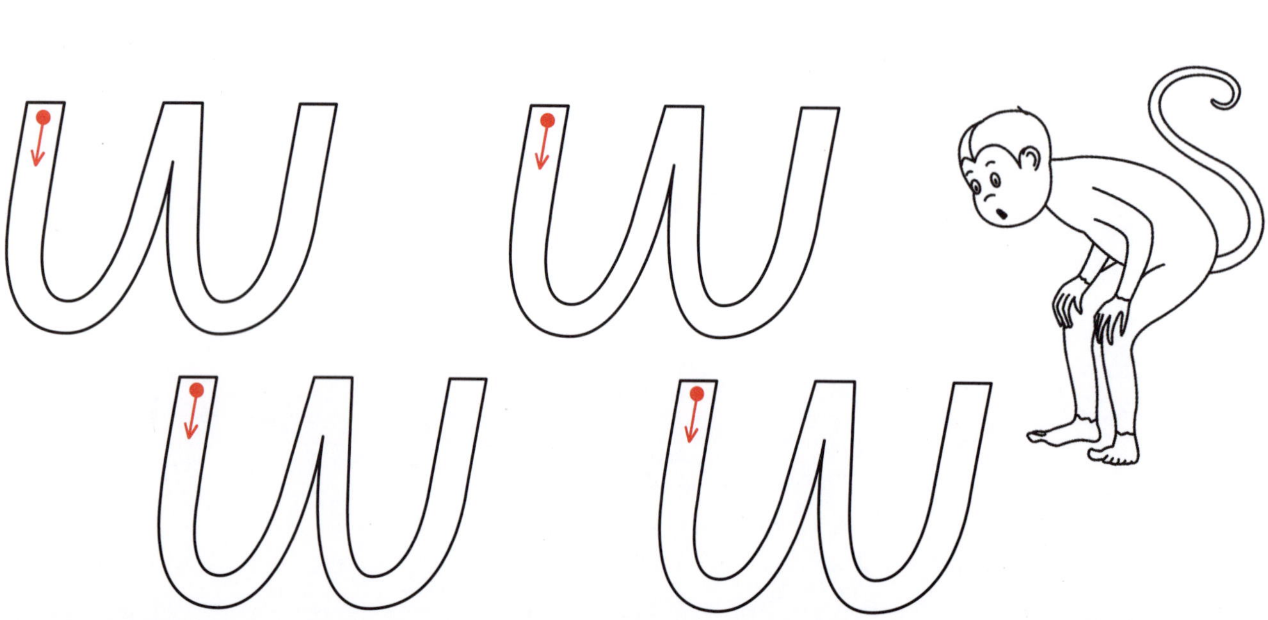

Start at the red dots. Follow the arrows.

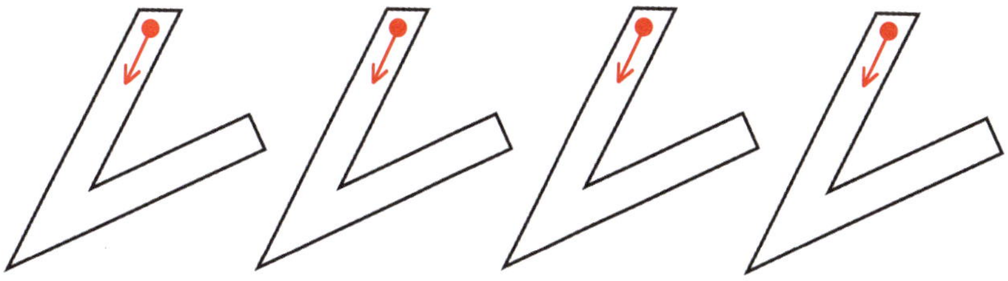

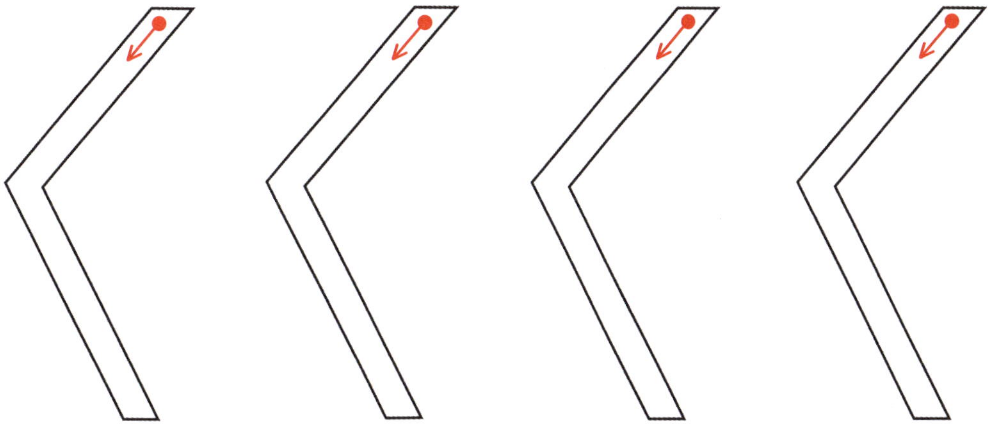

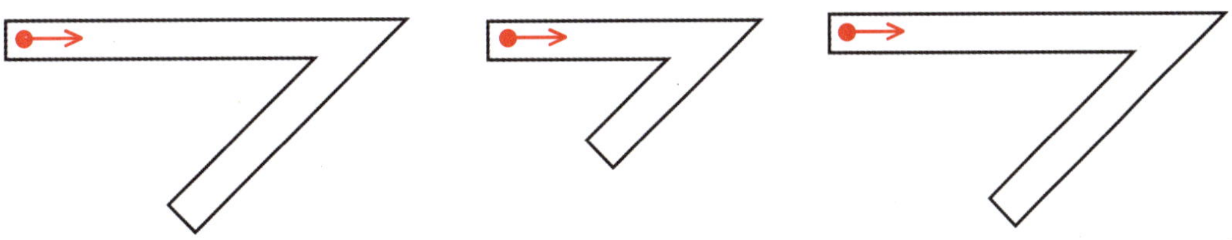

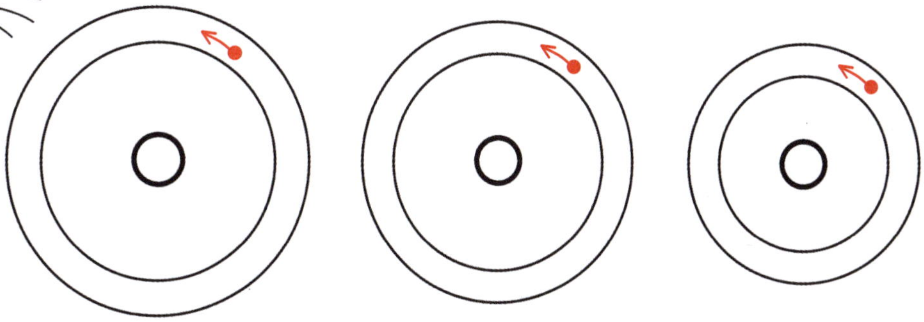

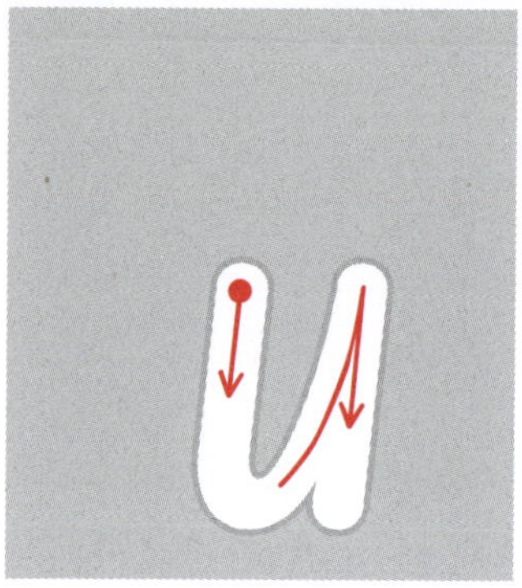

umbrella

Start at the dot. Follow the arrow.

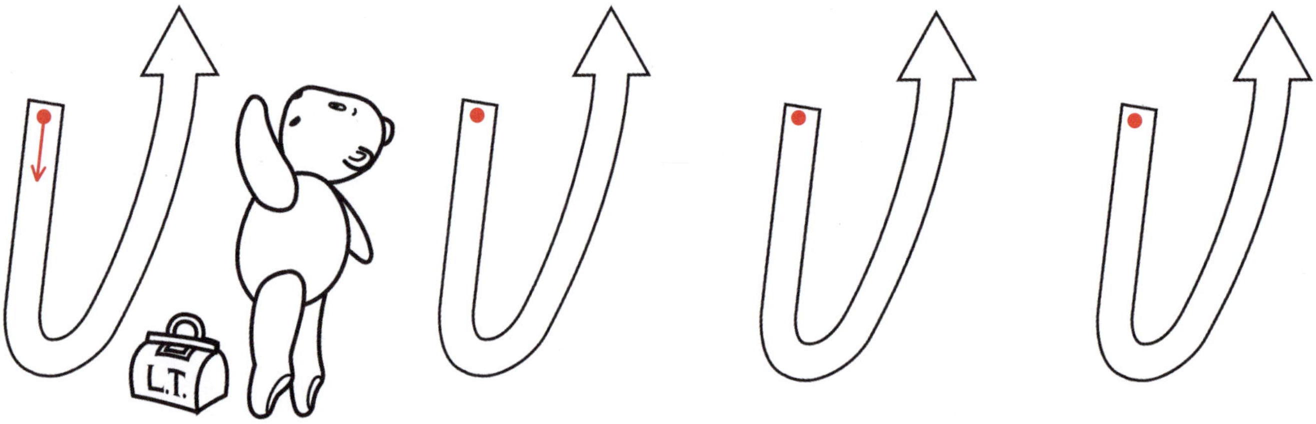

up

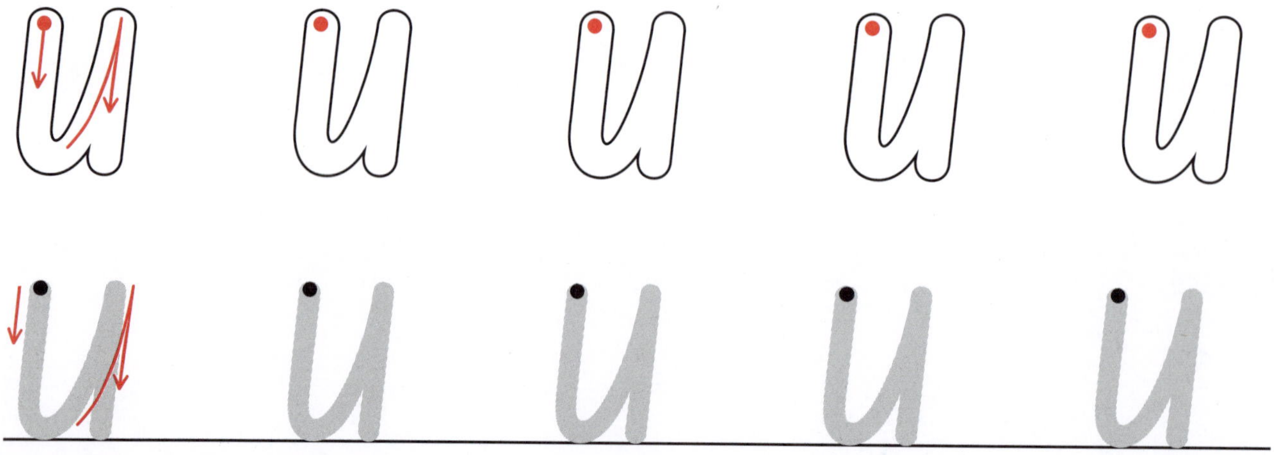

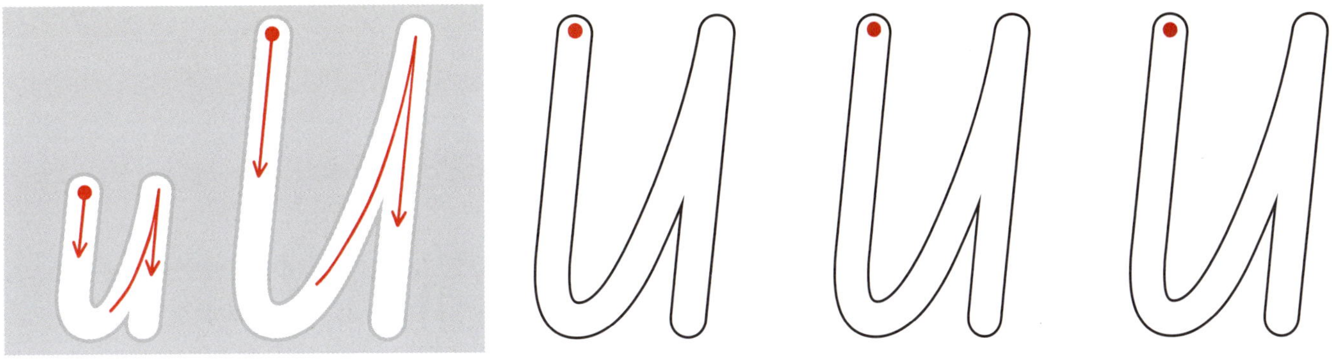

upstairs

umbrella

Trace the letter.

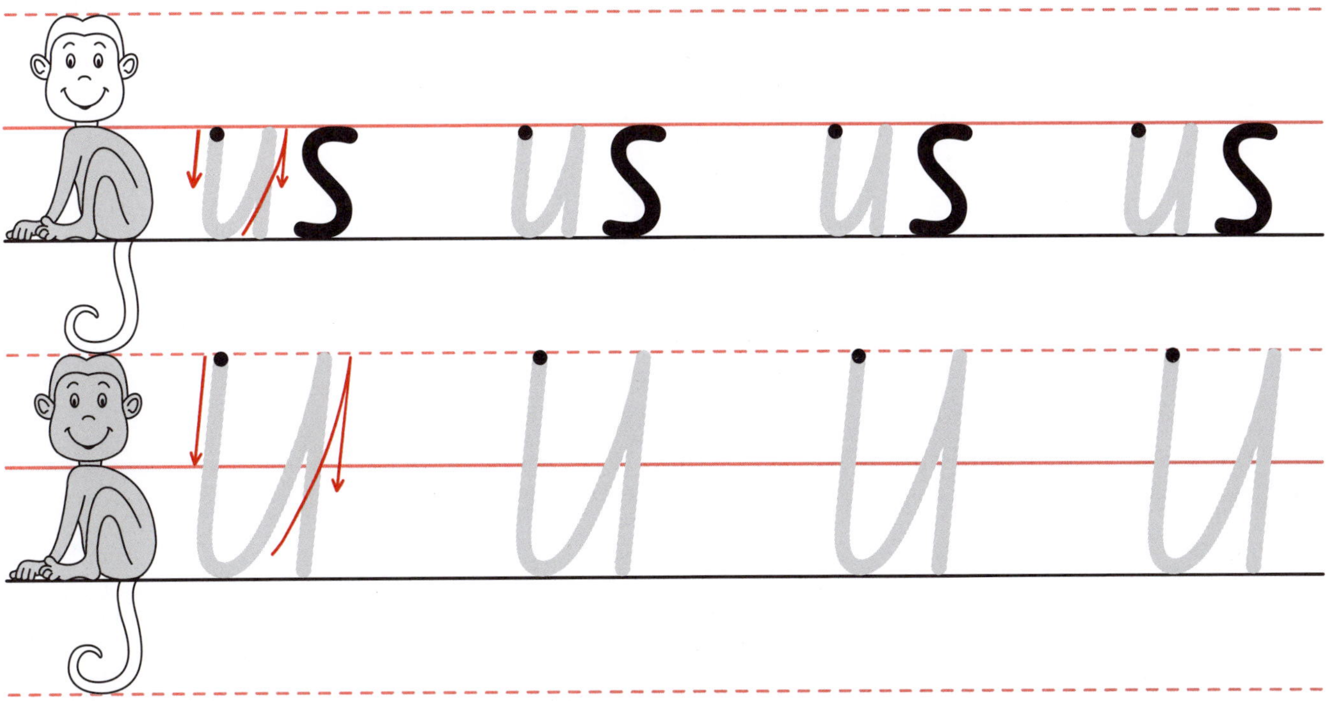

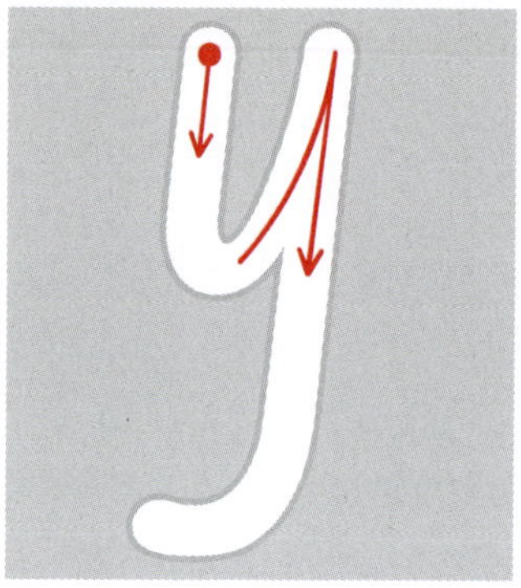

yo-yo

Start at the dot. Follow the arrow.

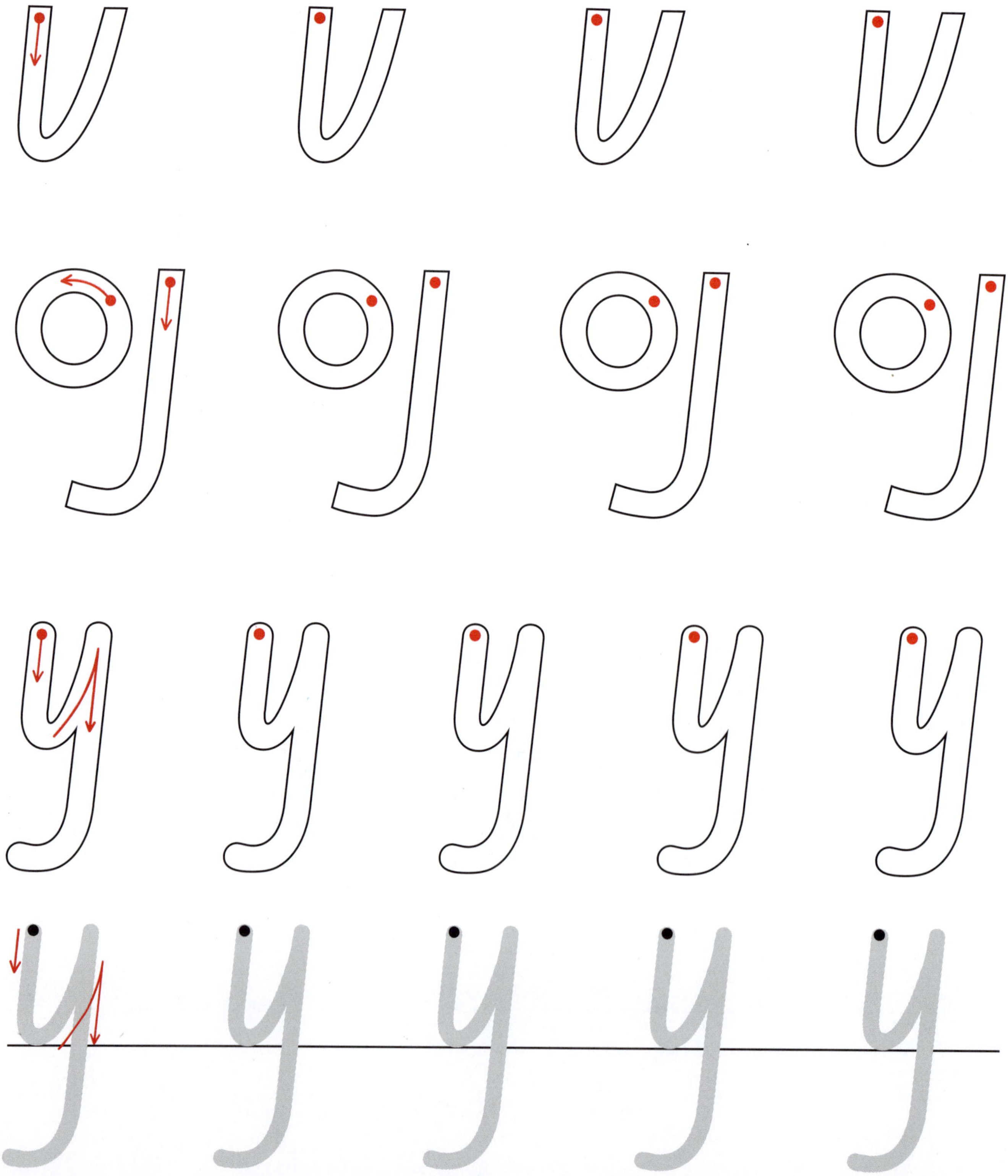

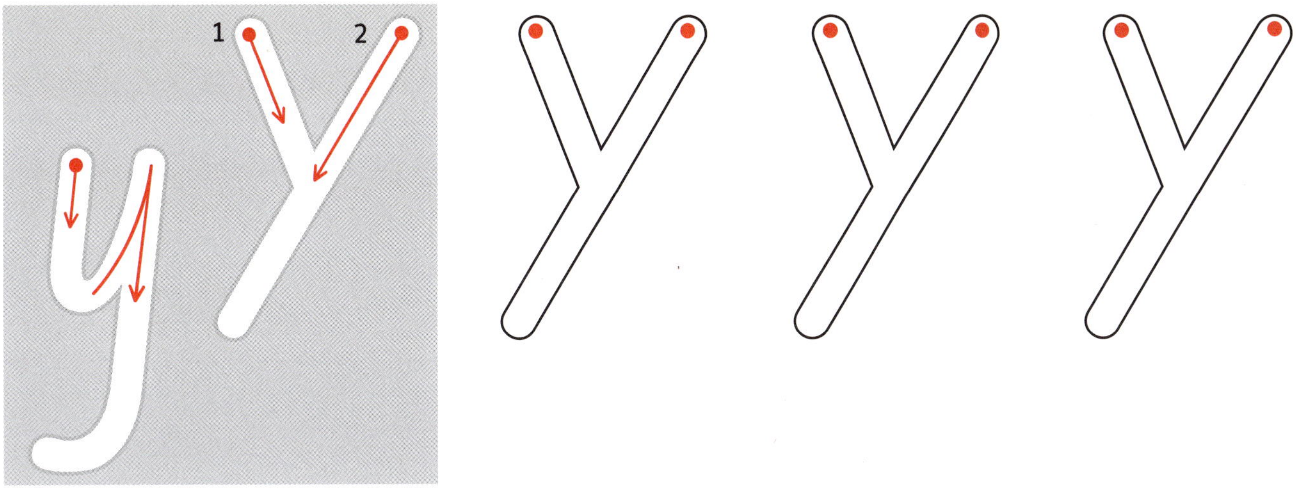

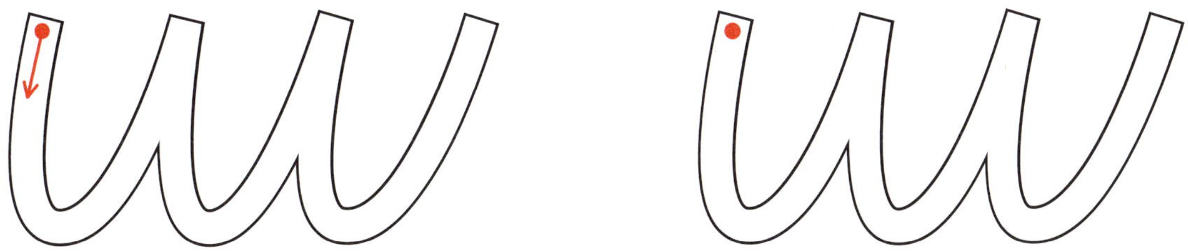

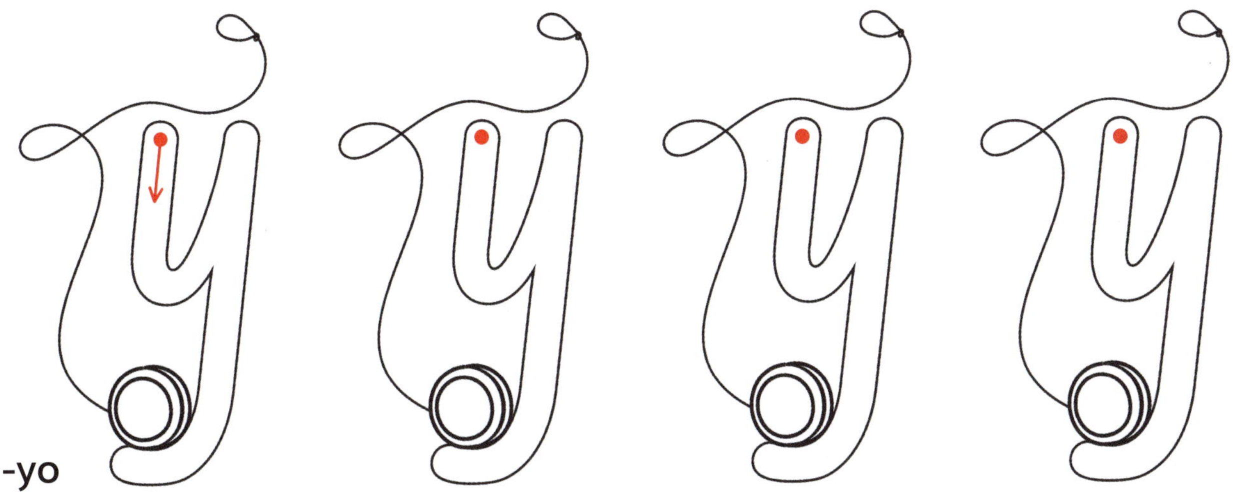

yo-yo

Trace the letter.

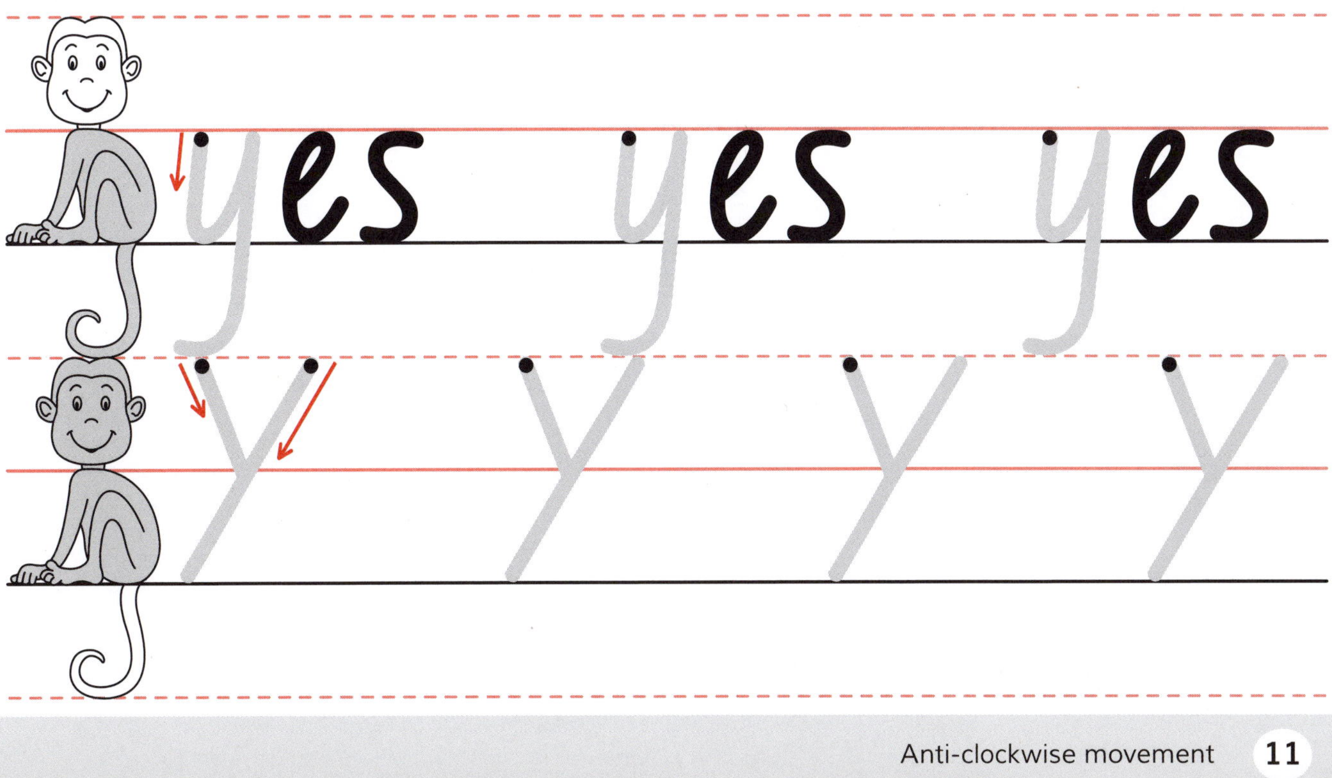

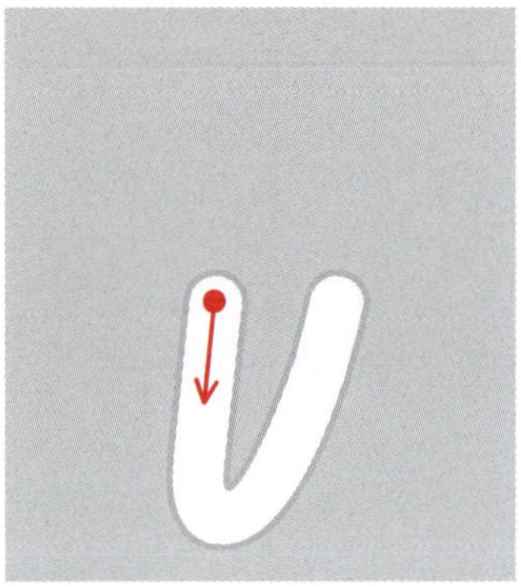

van

Start at the dot. Follow the arrow.

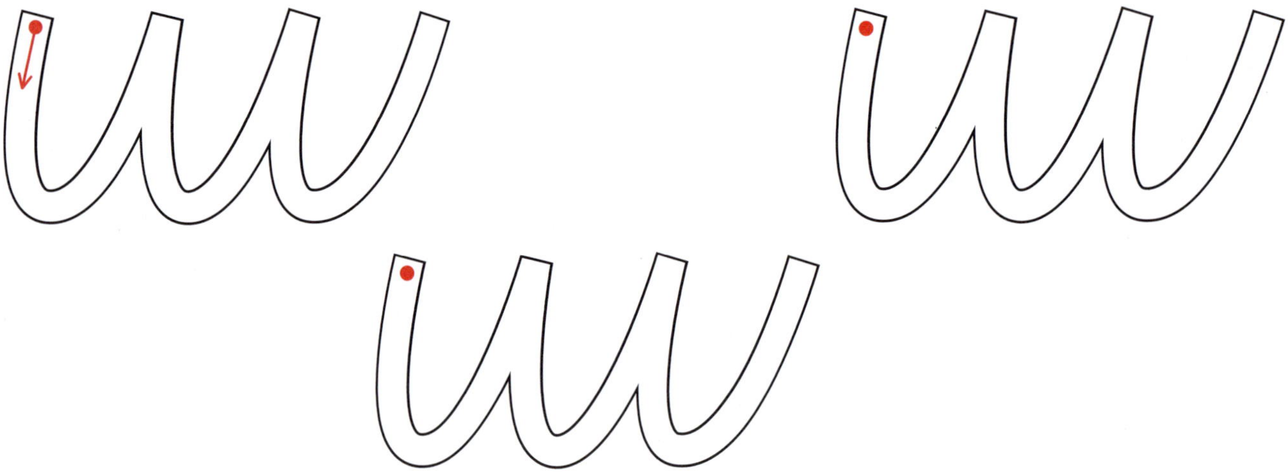

volcano

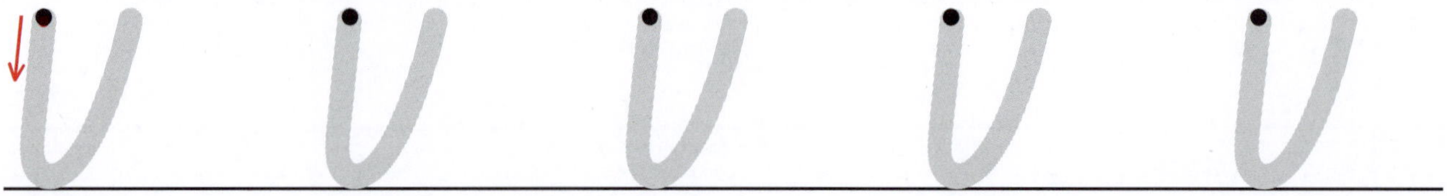

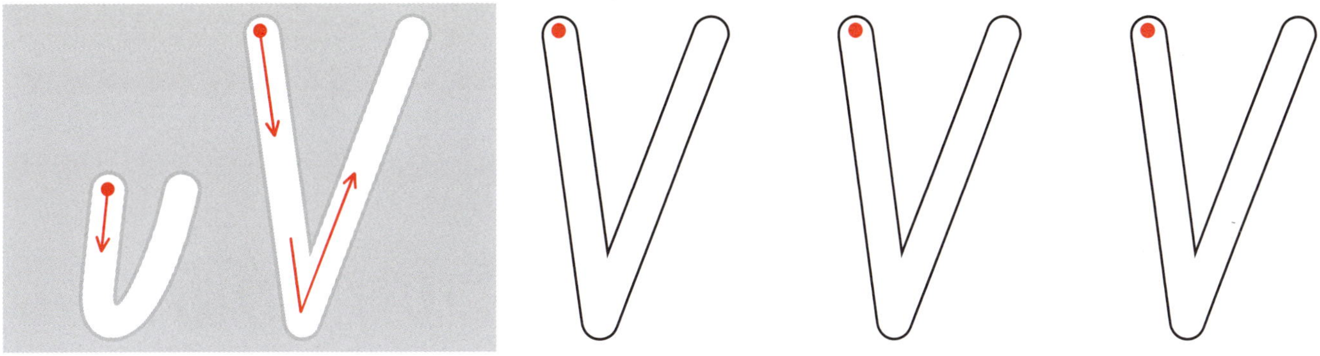

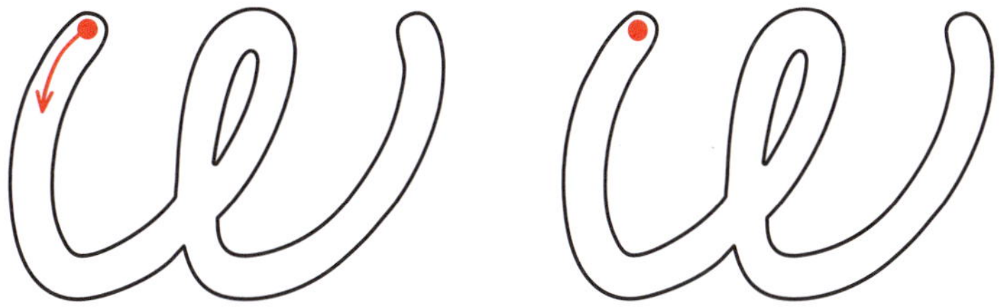

van

vase

Trace the letter.

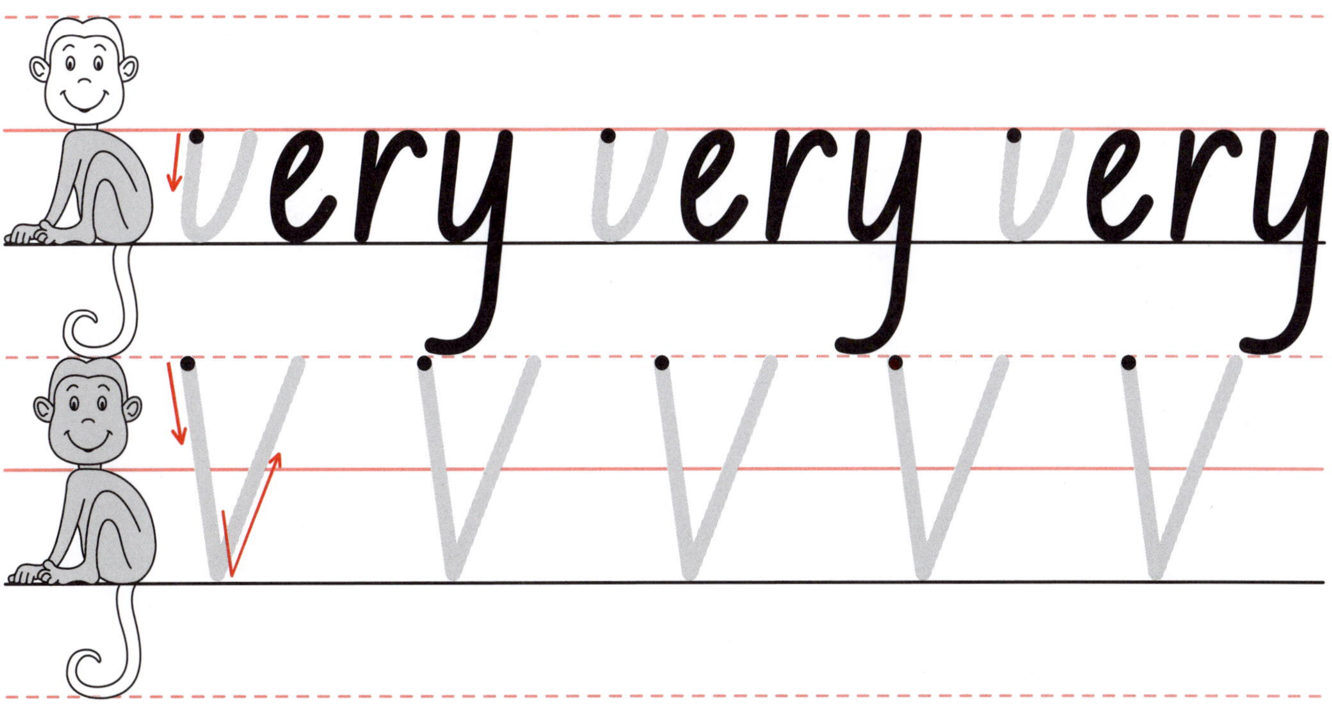

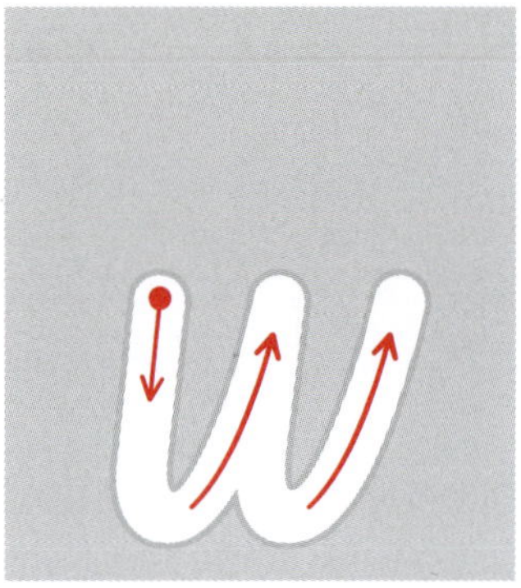

window

Start at the dot. Follow the arrow.

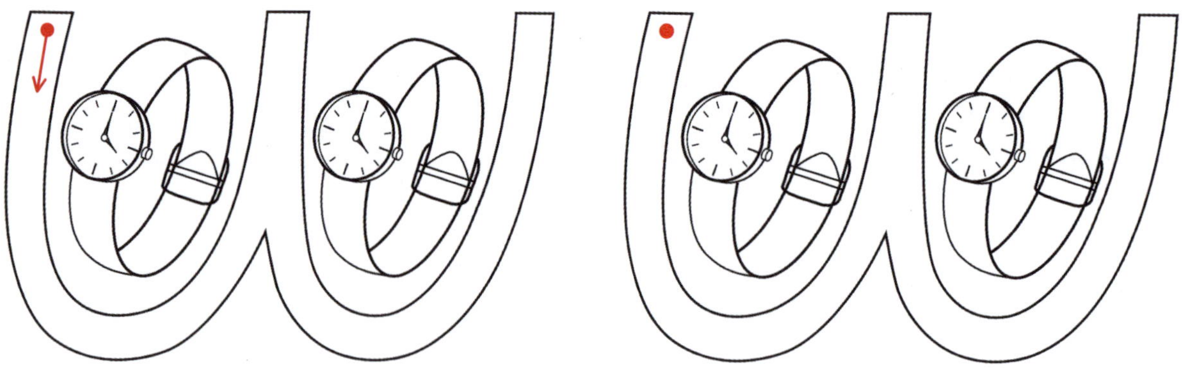

watches

waves

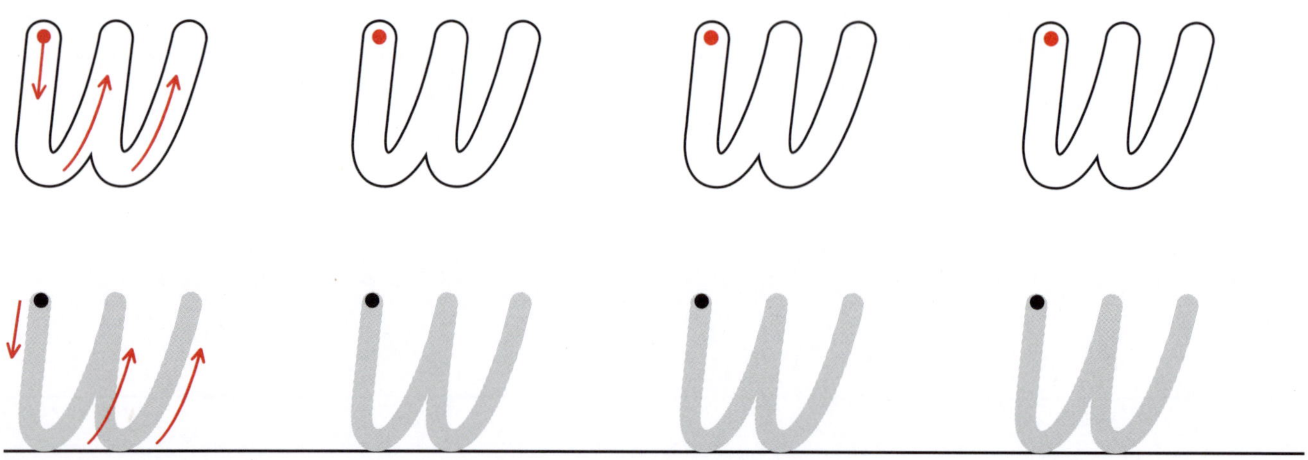

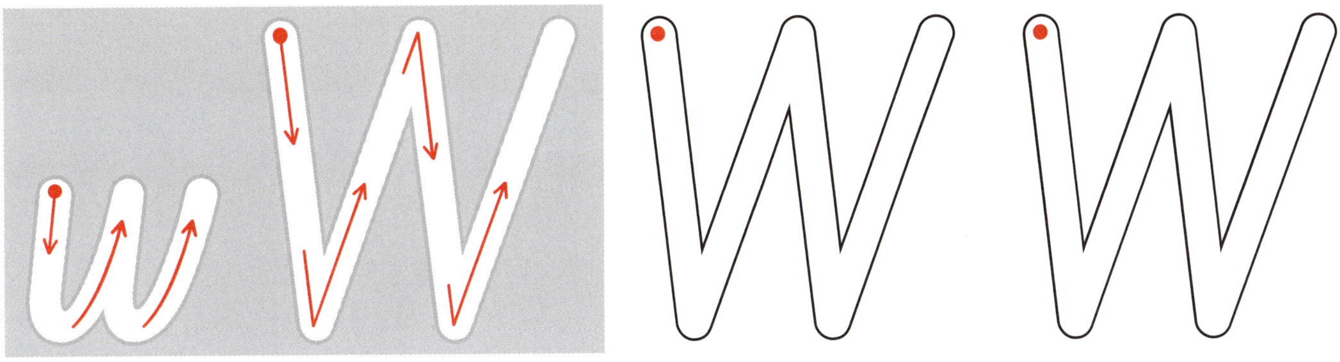

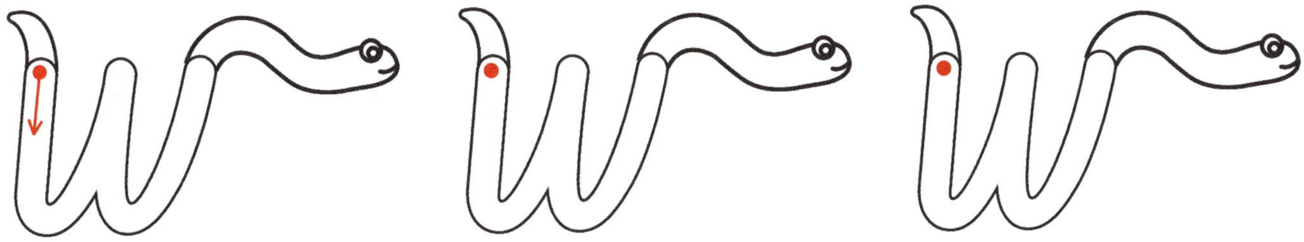

worm

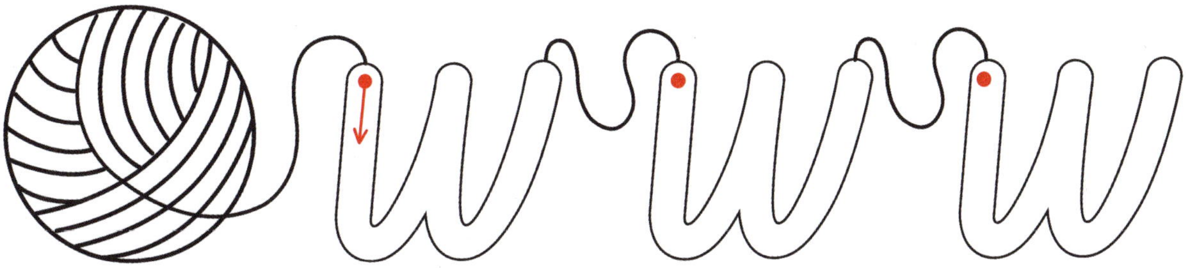

wool

Trace the letter.

get.ga/PMWA41

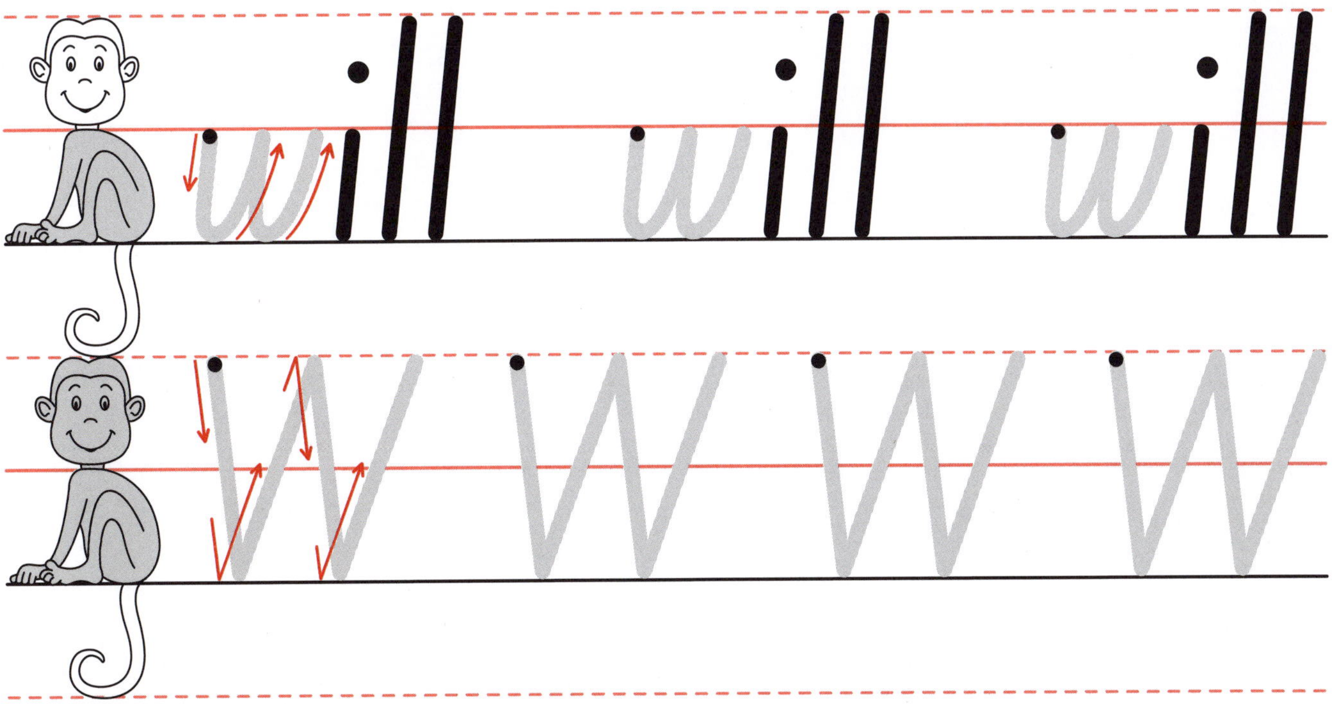

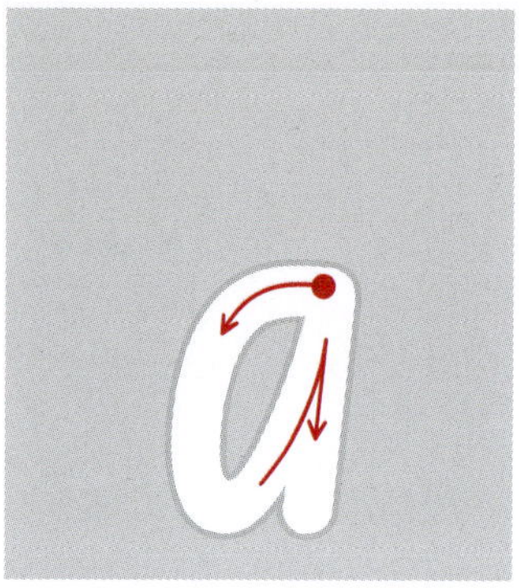

apple

Start at the dot. Follow the arrow.

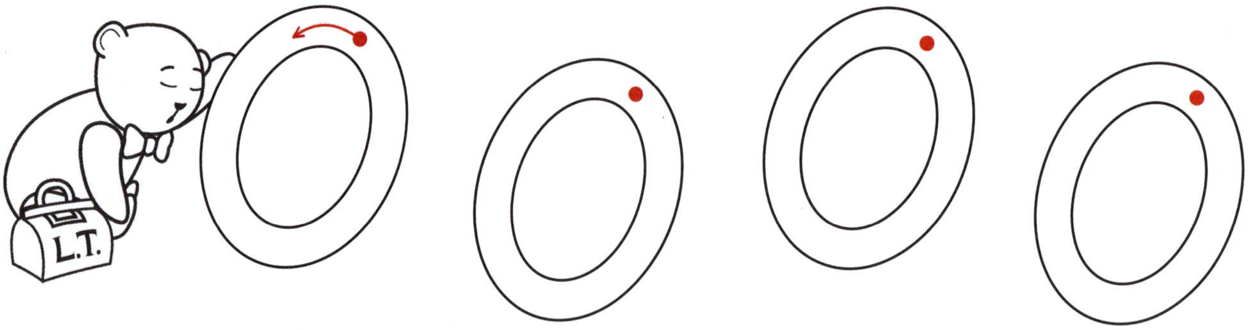

asleep

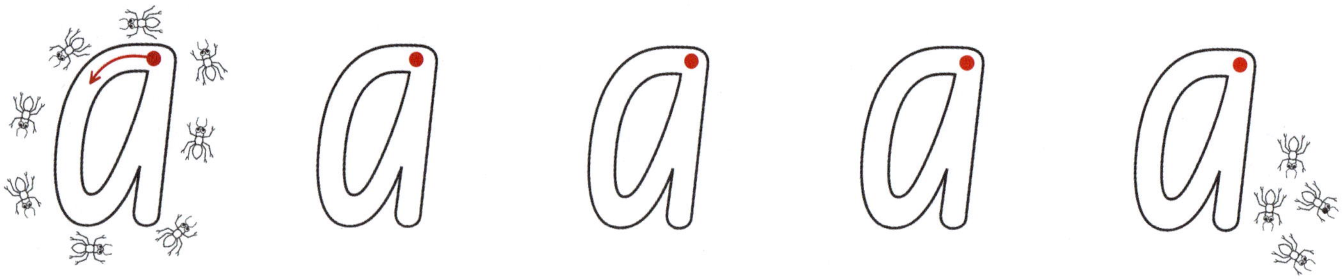

ants

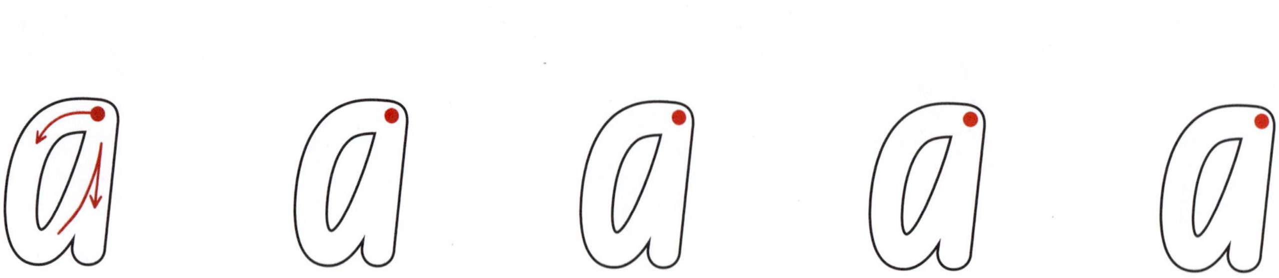

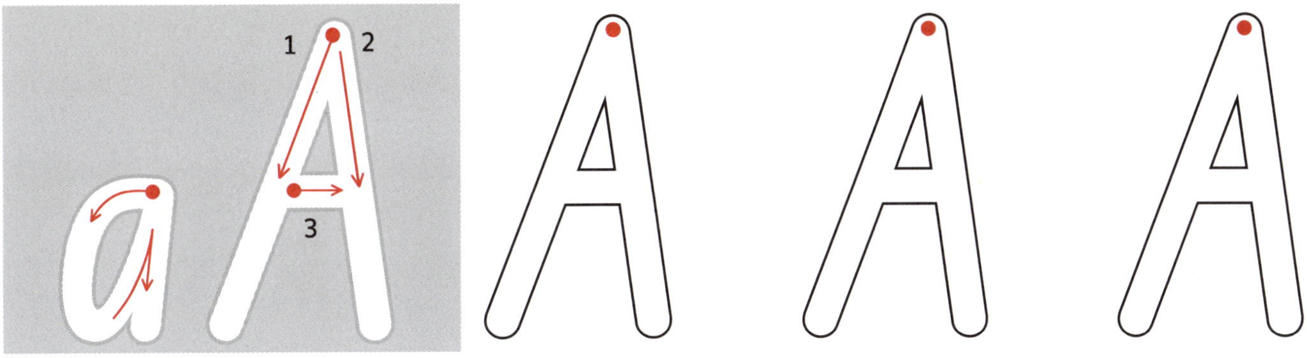

apple

Trace the letter.

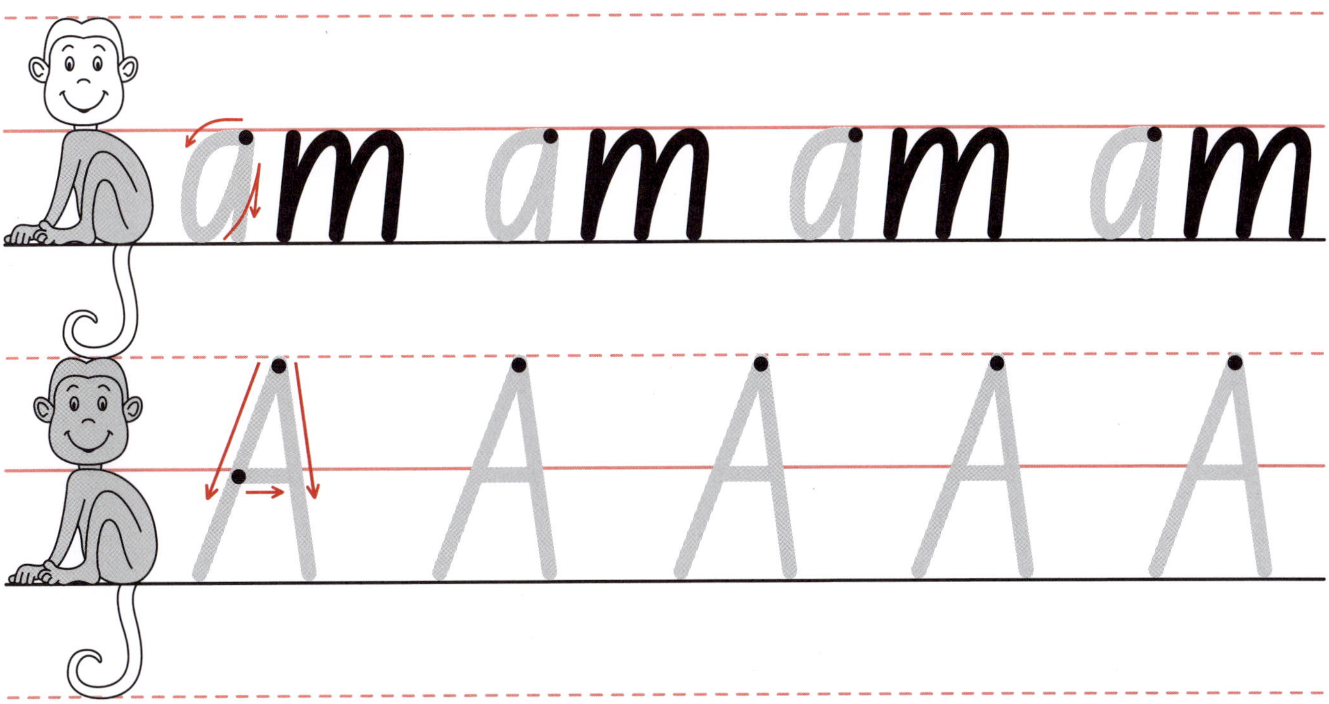

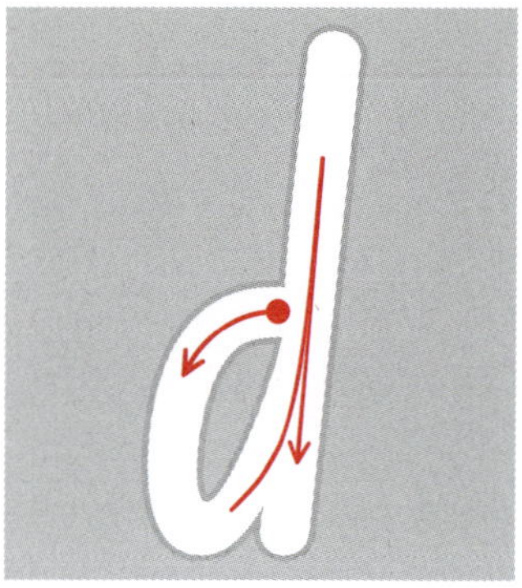

duck

Start at the dot. Follow the arrow.

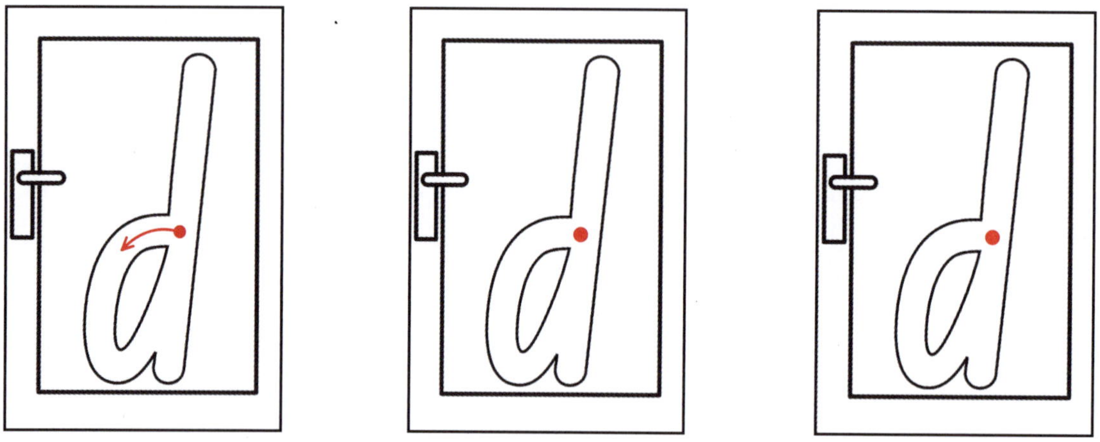

door

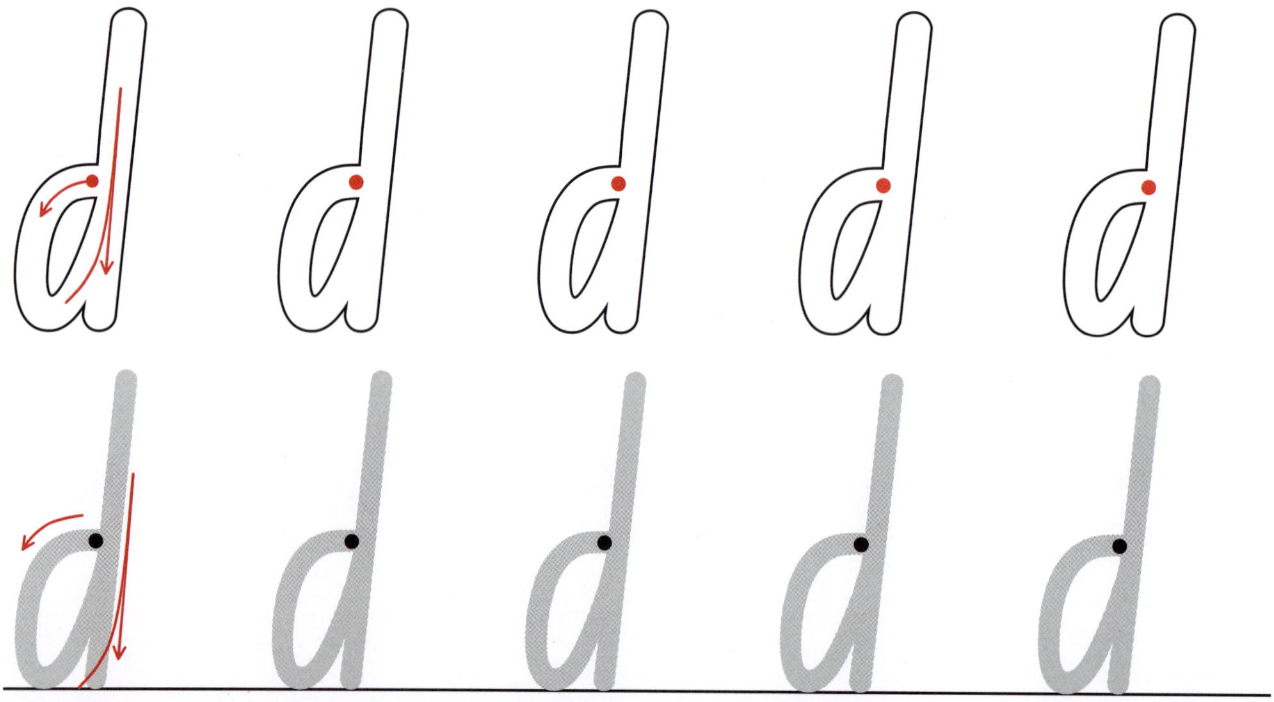

dog

dinosaur

Trace the letter.

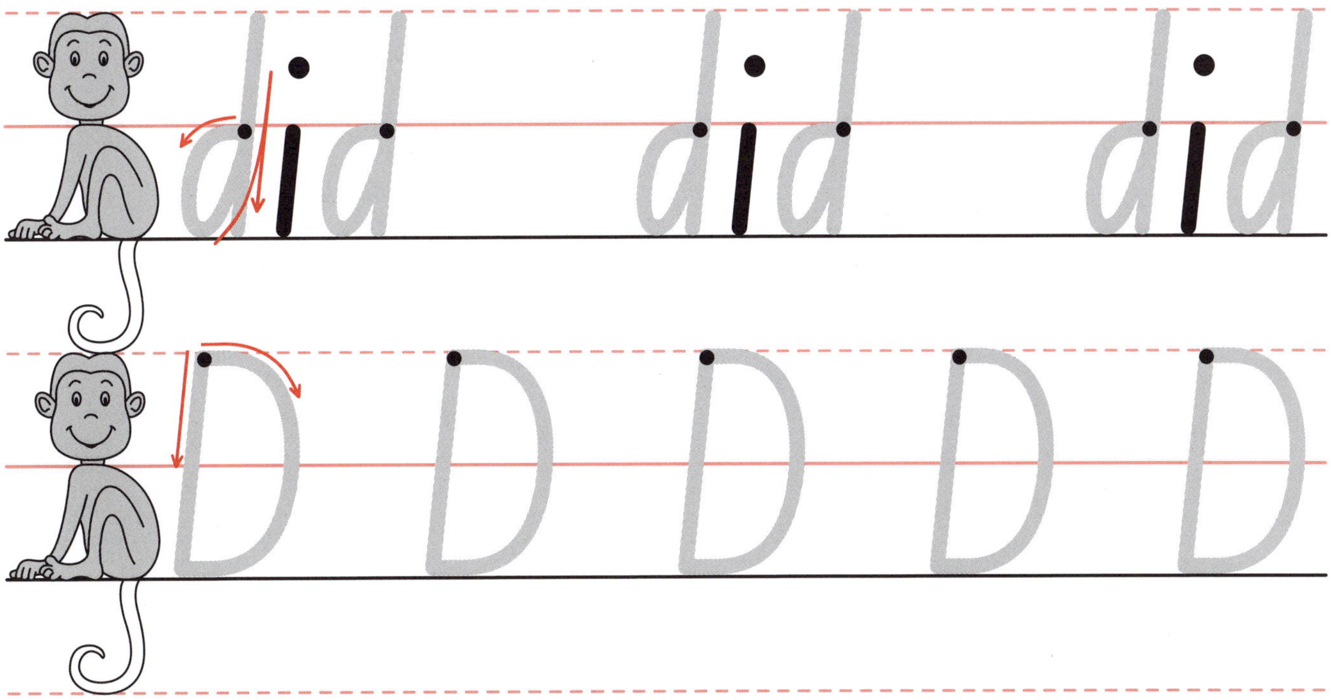

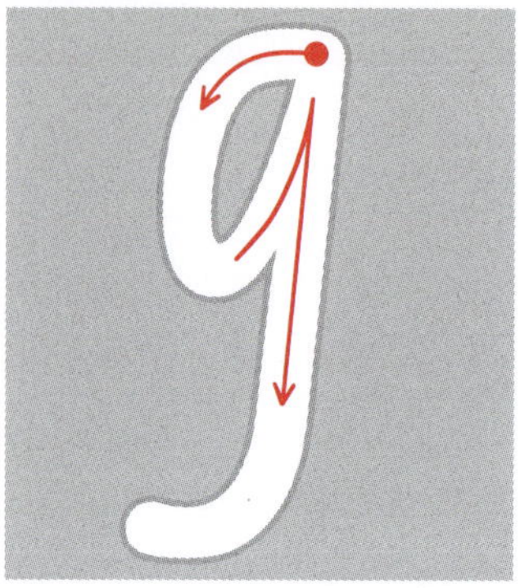

gate

Start at the dot. Follow the arrow.

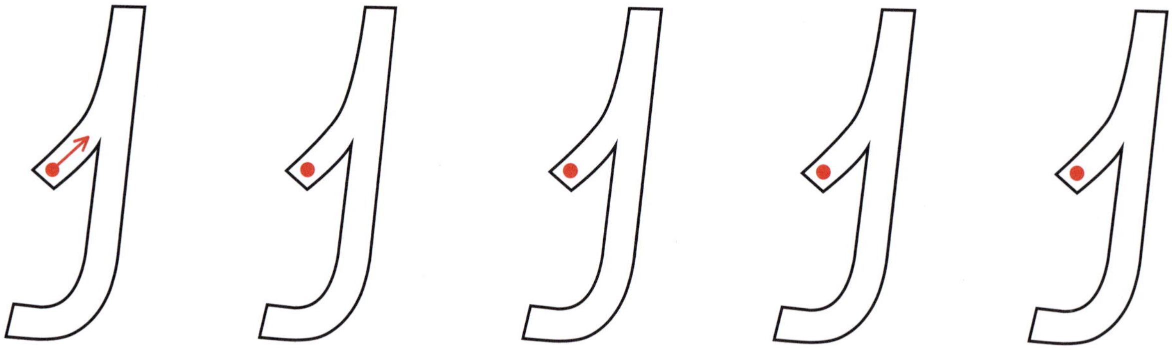

garden

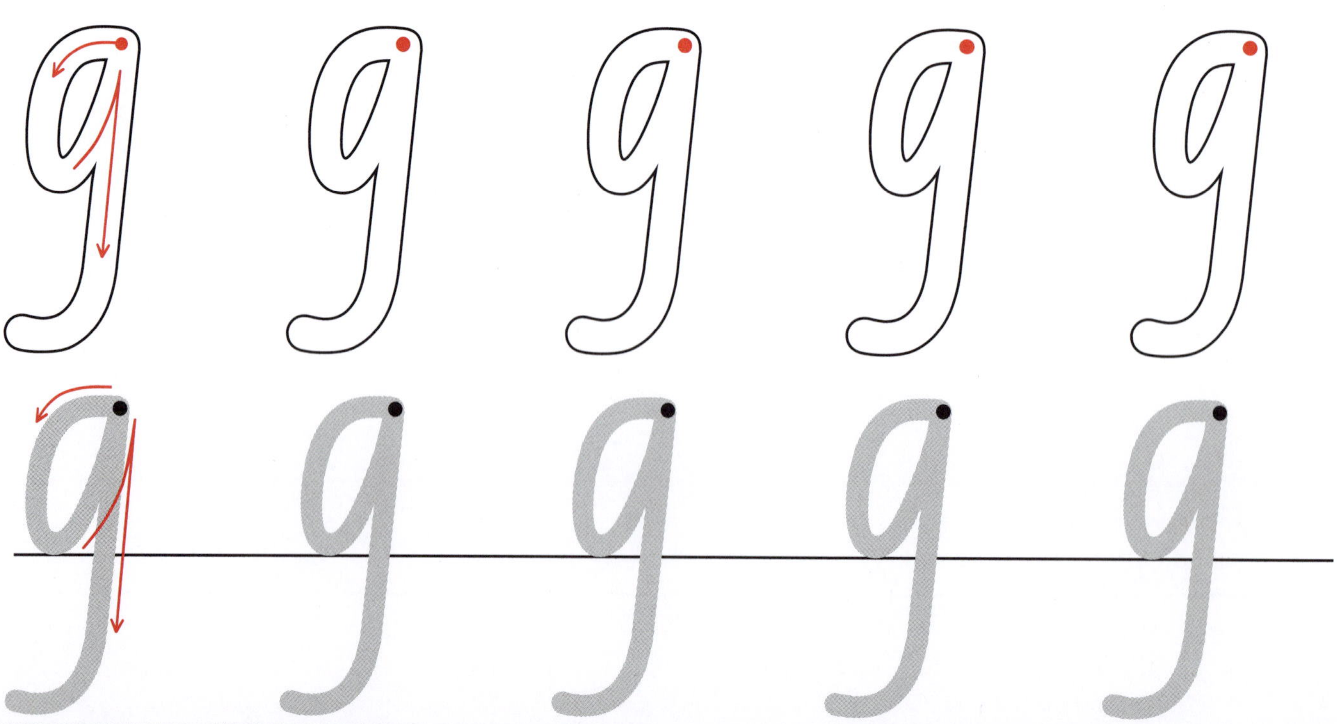

g G

G G G

g g g g

goat

g g g g

g

girl

Trace the letter.

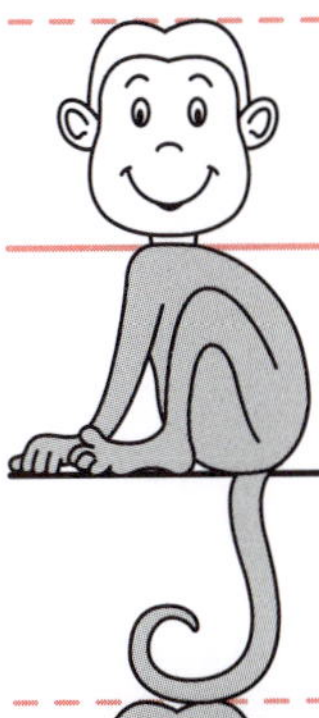

get get get get

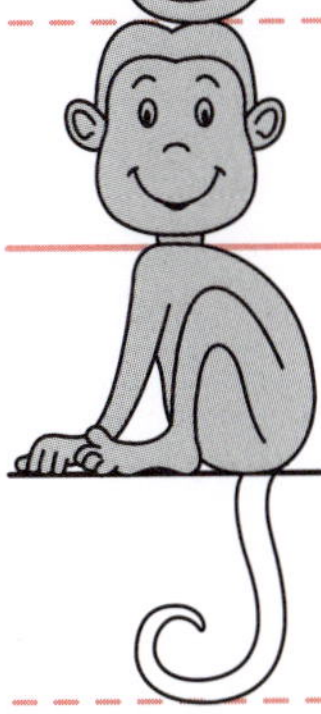

G G G G G

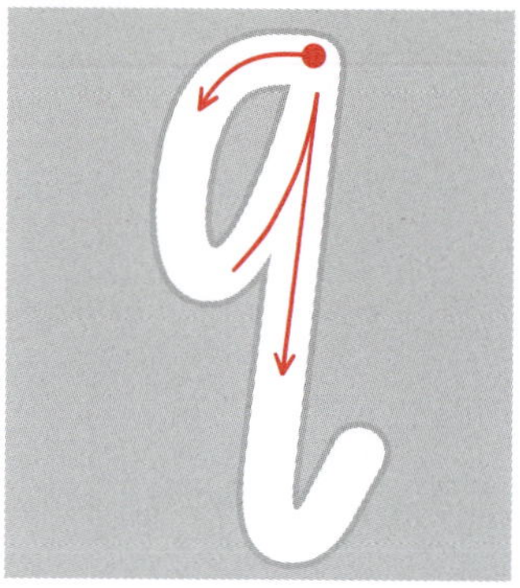

queen

Start at the dot. Follow the arrow.

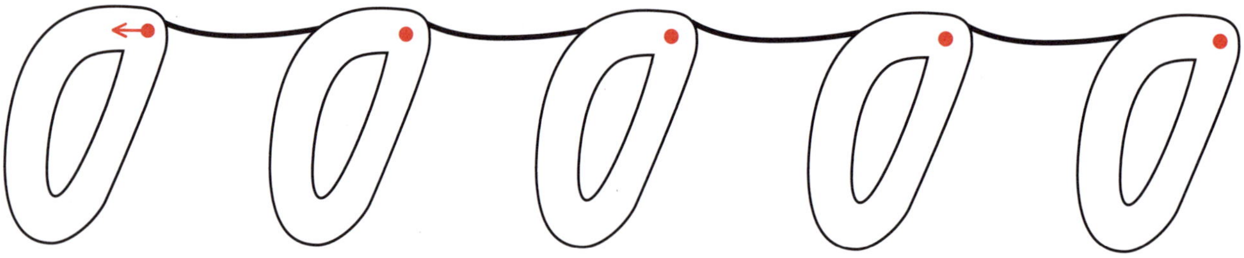

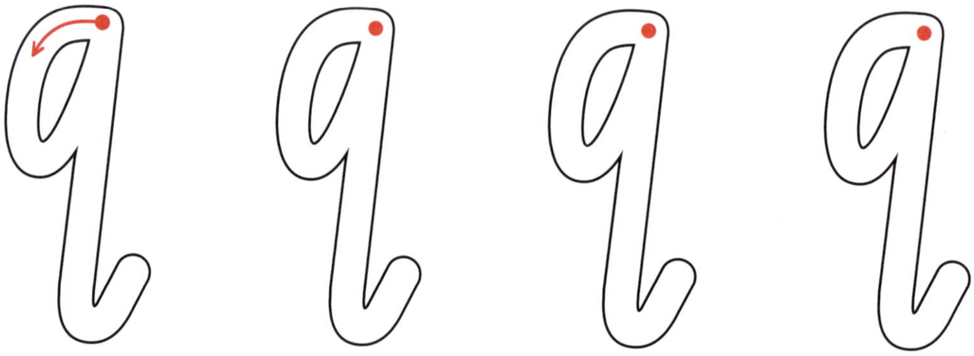

queen

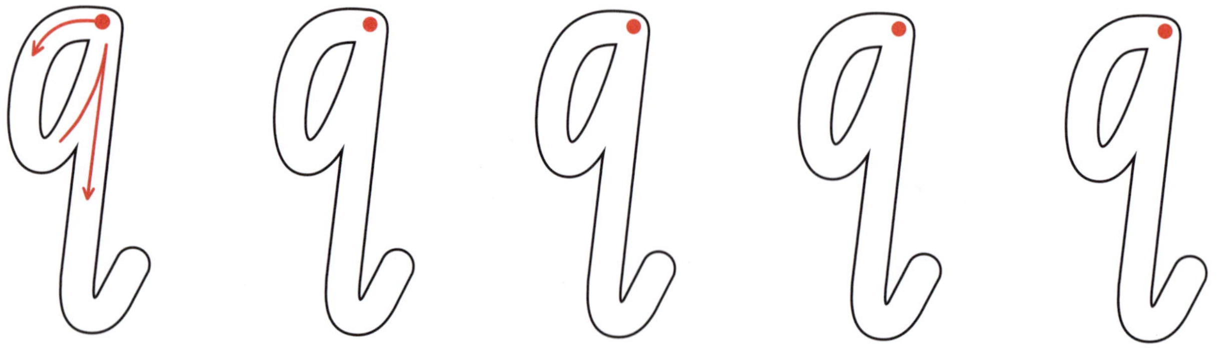

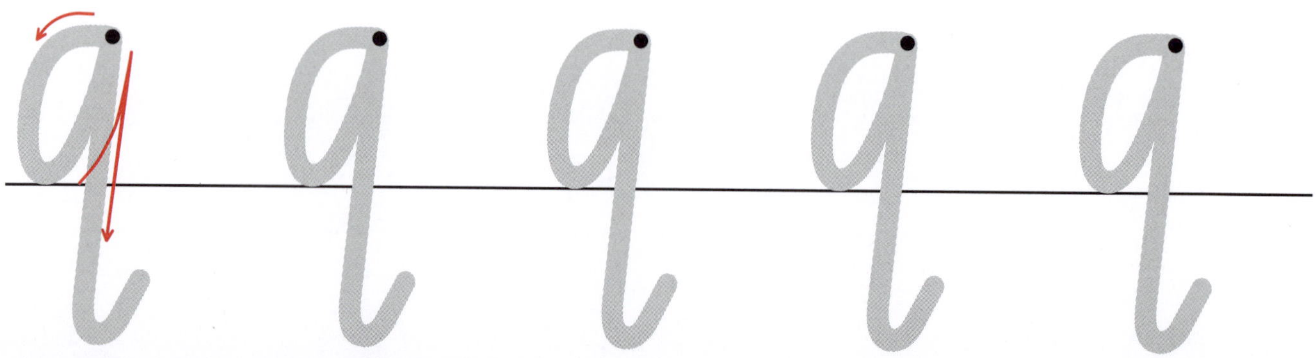

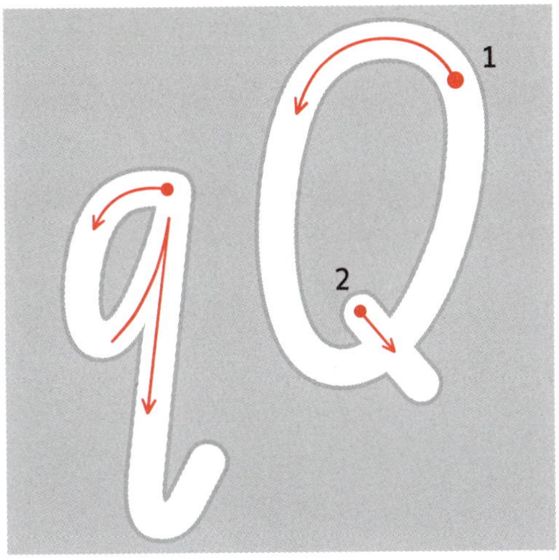

question mark

get.ga/PMWA42

Trace the letter.

quick quick

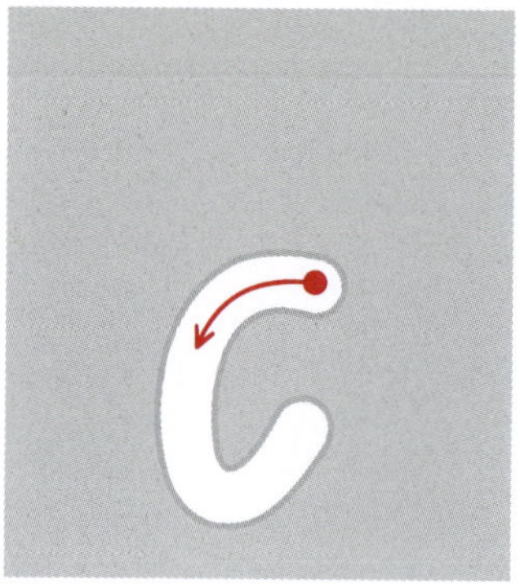

caterpillar

Start at the dot. Follow the arrow.

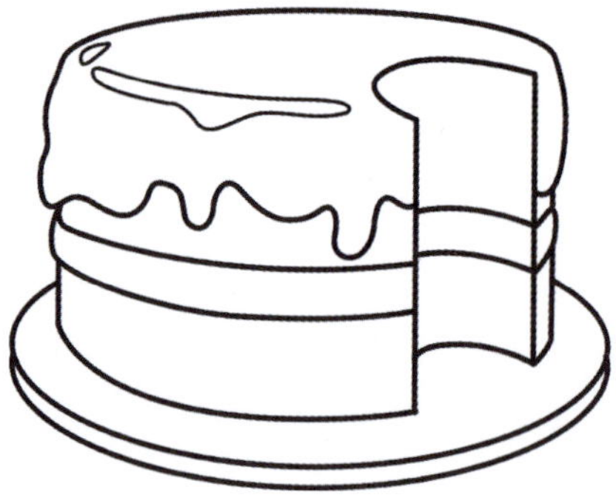

cake

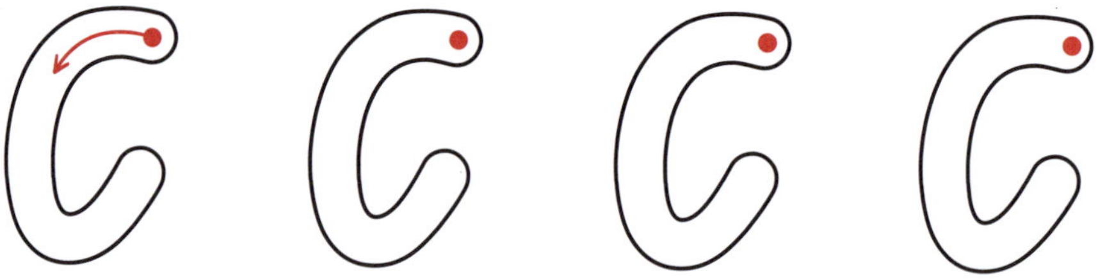

cat

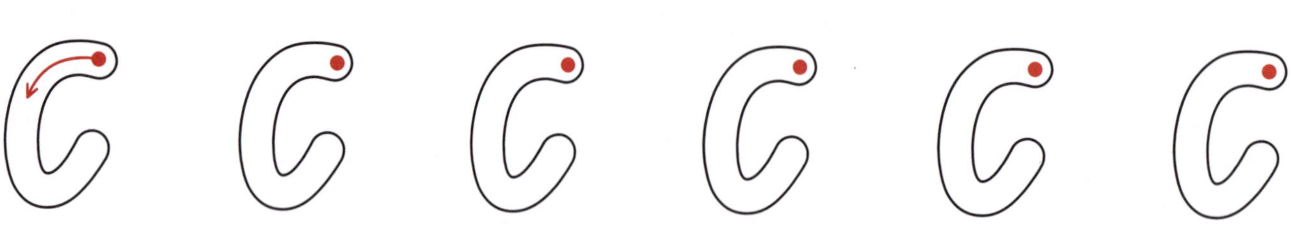

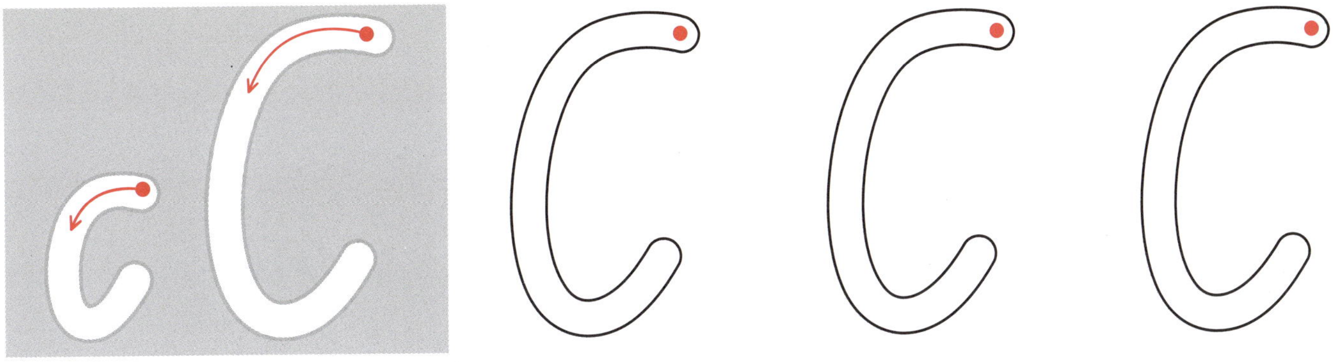

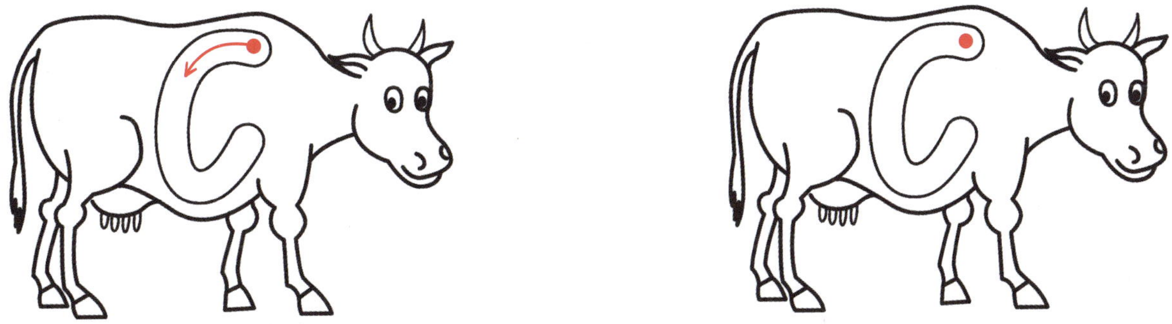

cow

car

Trace the letter.

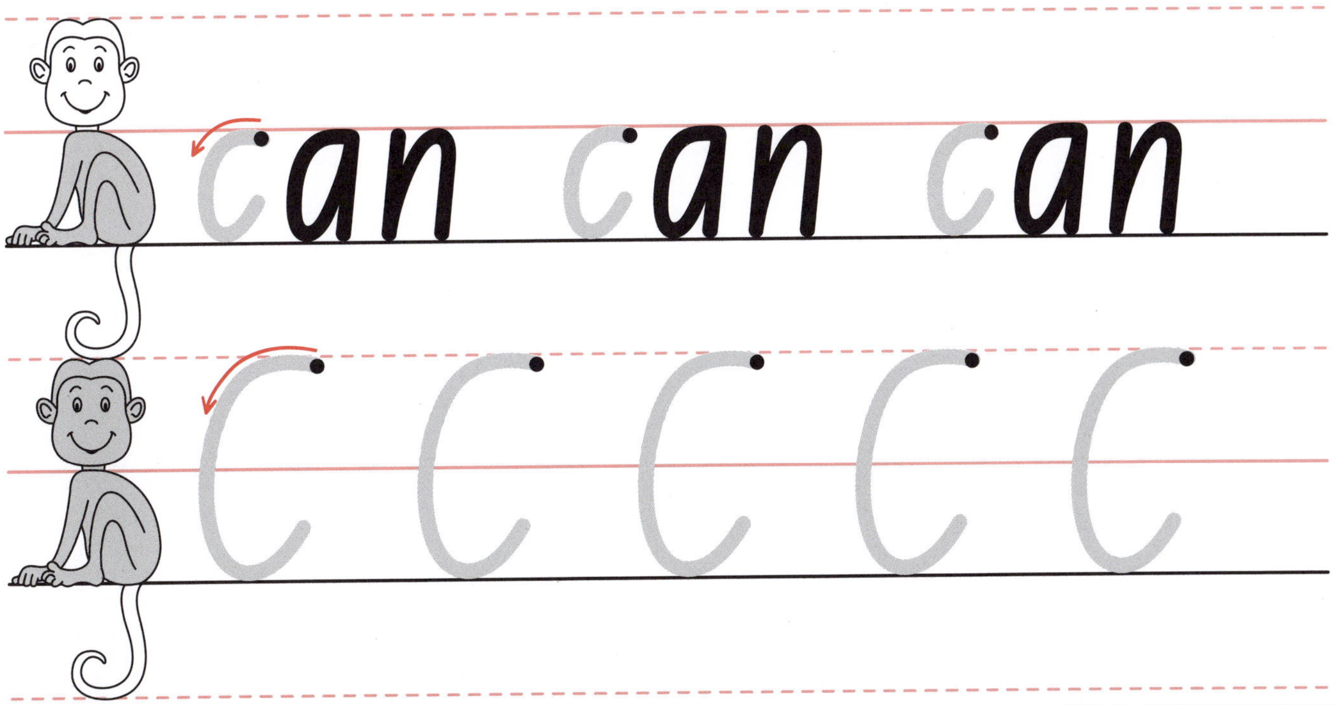

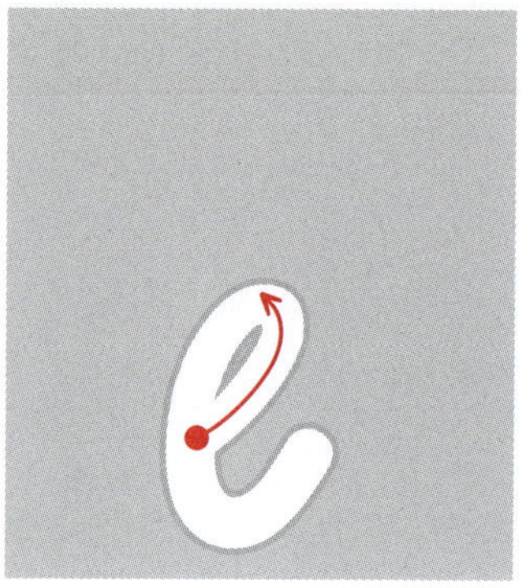

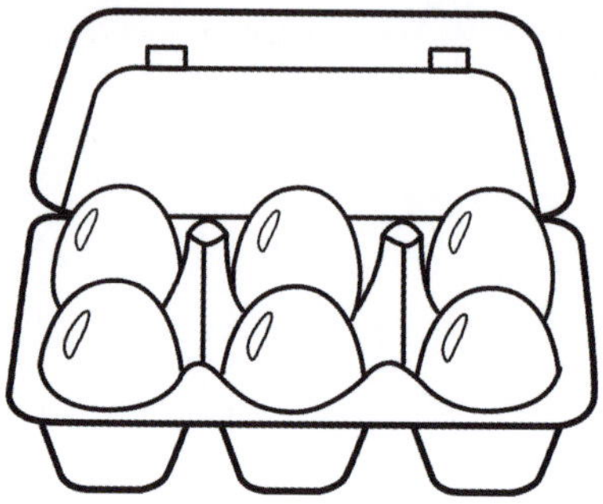

eggs

Start at the dot. Follow the arrow.

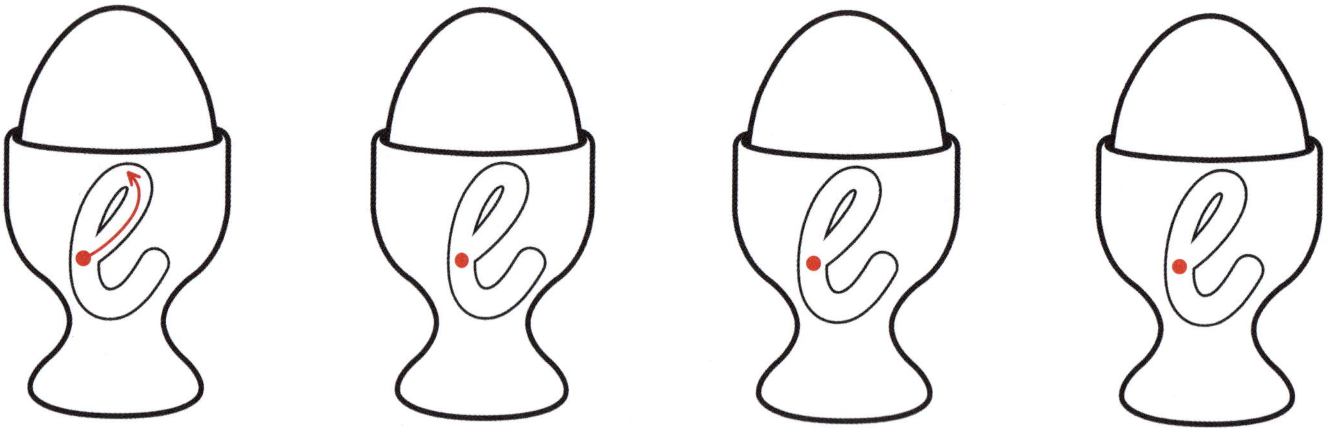

egg

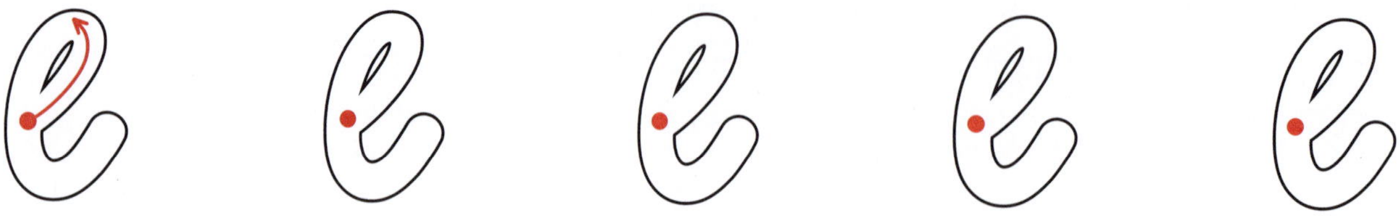

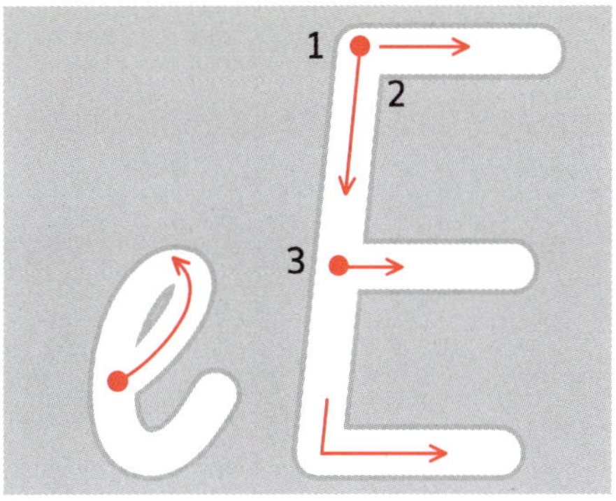

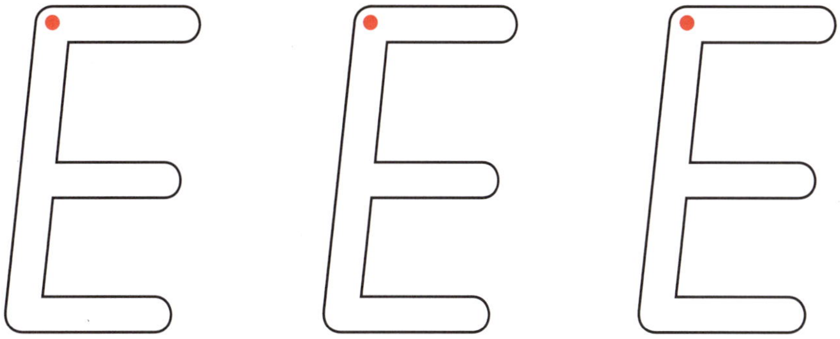

elephant

ear

Trace the letter.

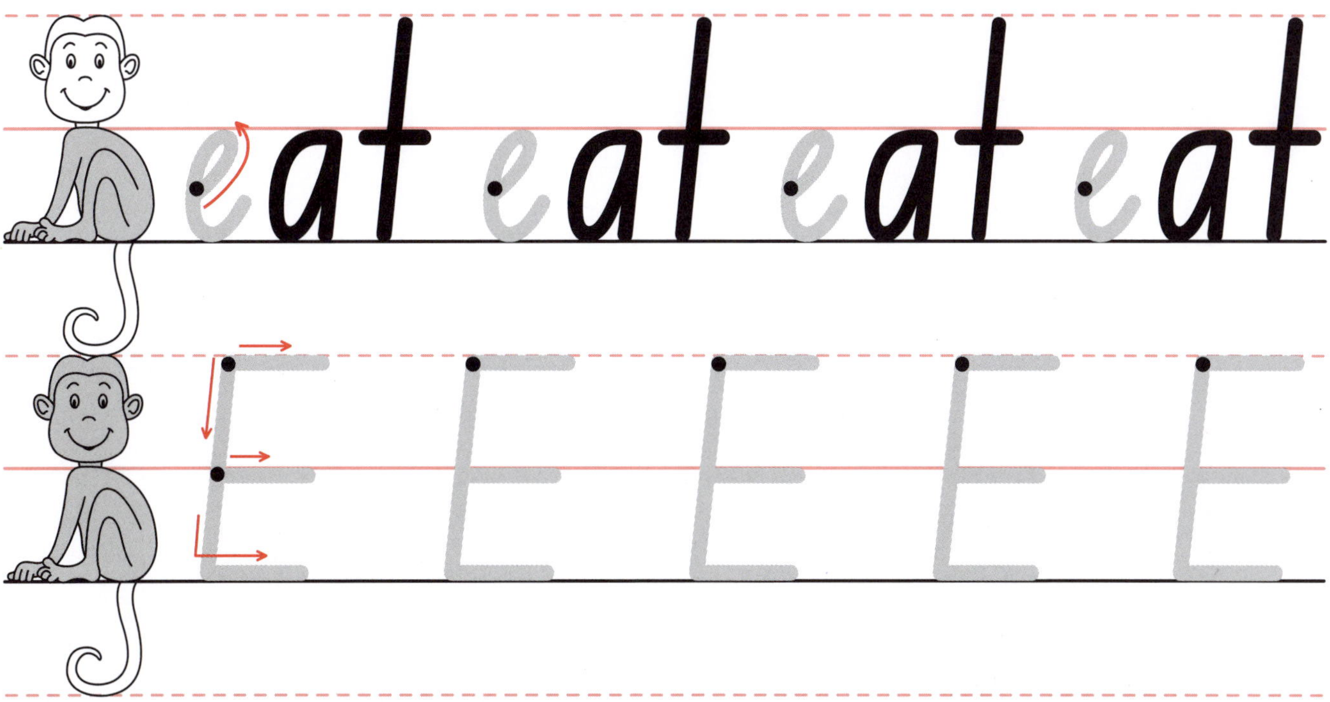

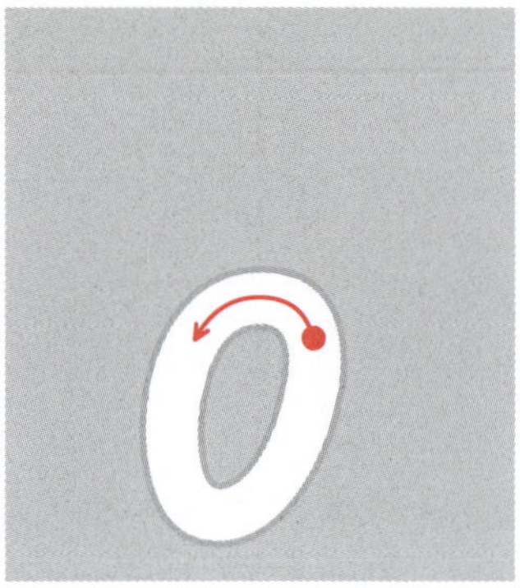

outside

Start at the dot. Follow the arrow.

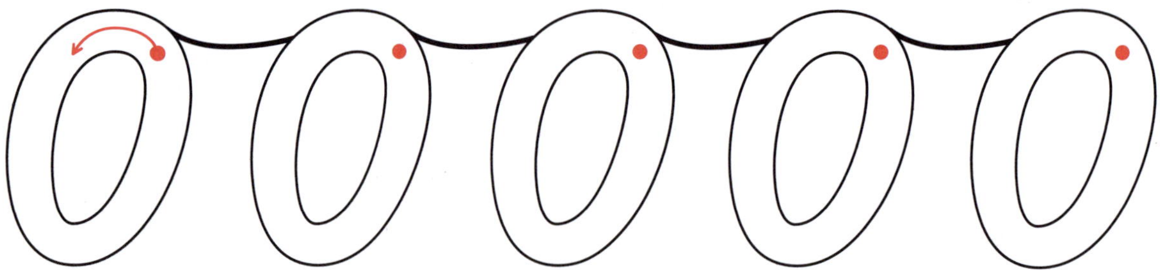

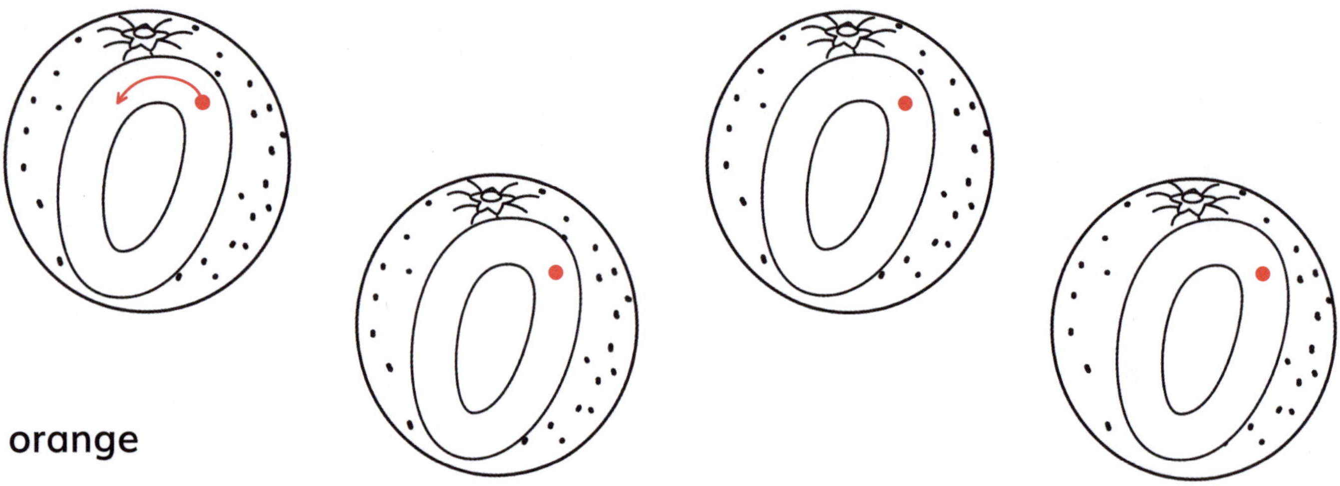

orange

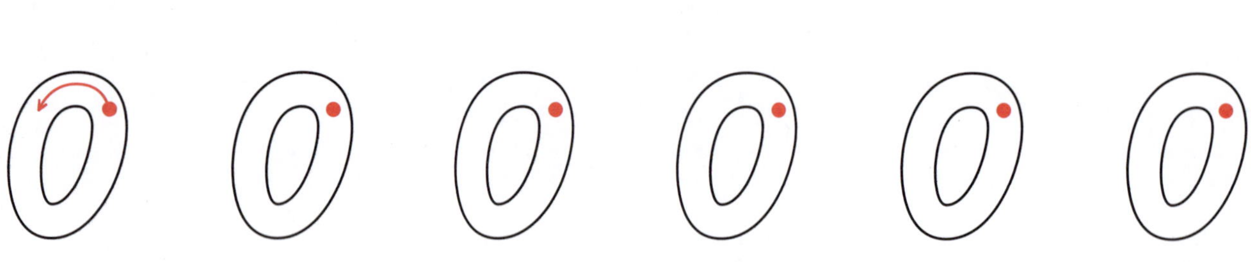

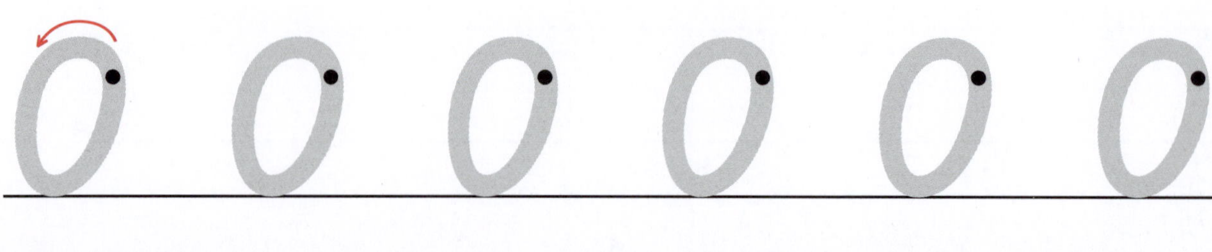

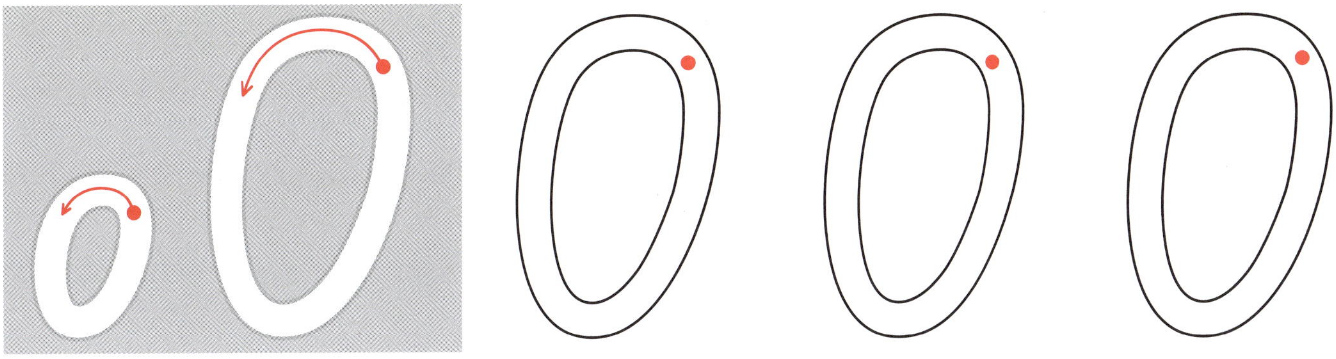

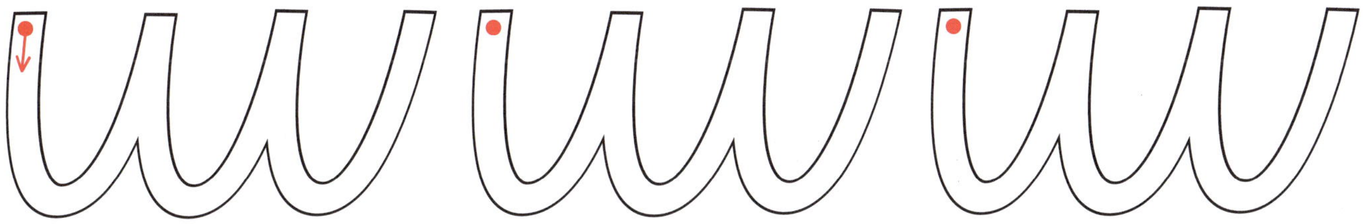

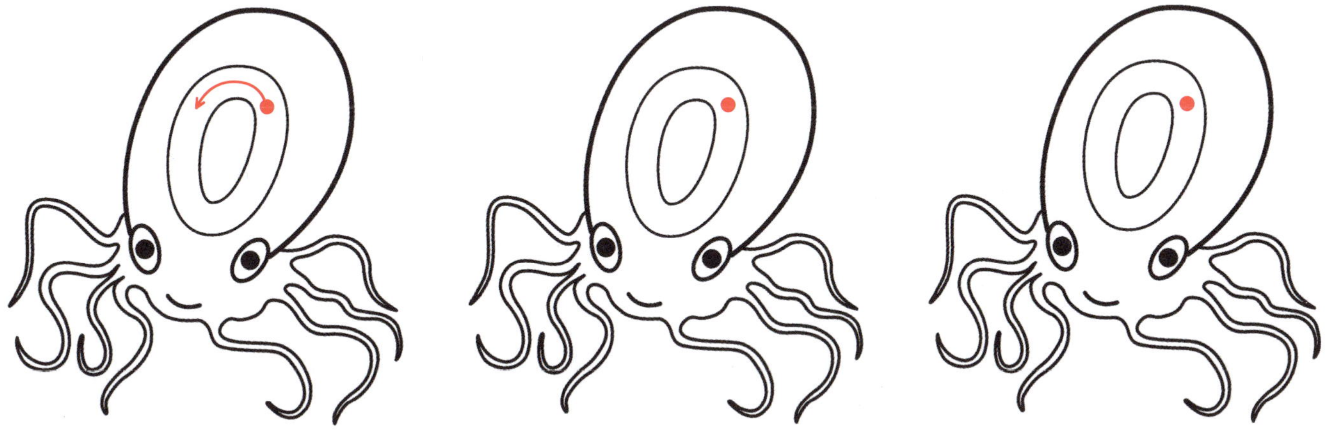

octopus

Trace the letter.

off off off

o o o o o

sun

Start at the dot. Follow the arrow.

snake

sun

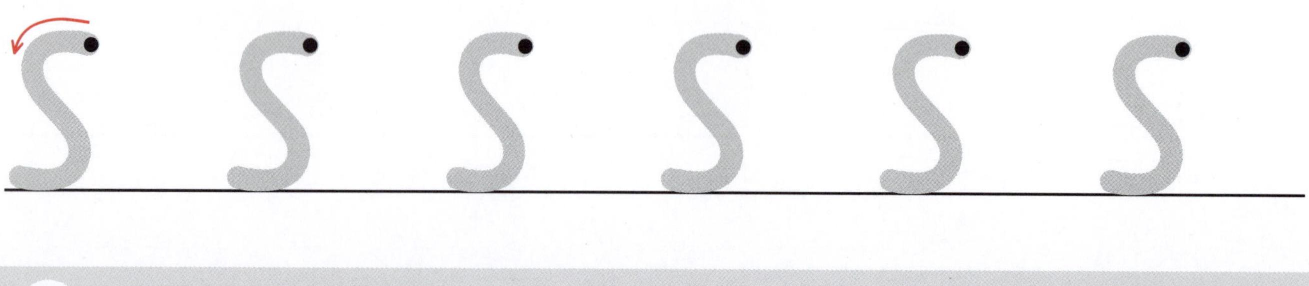

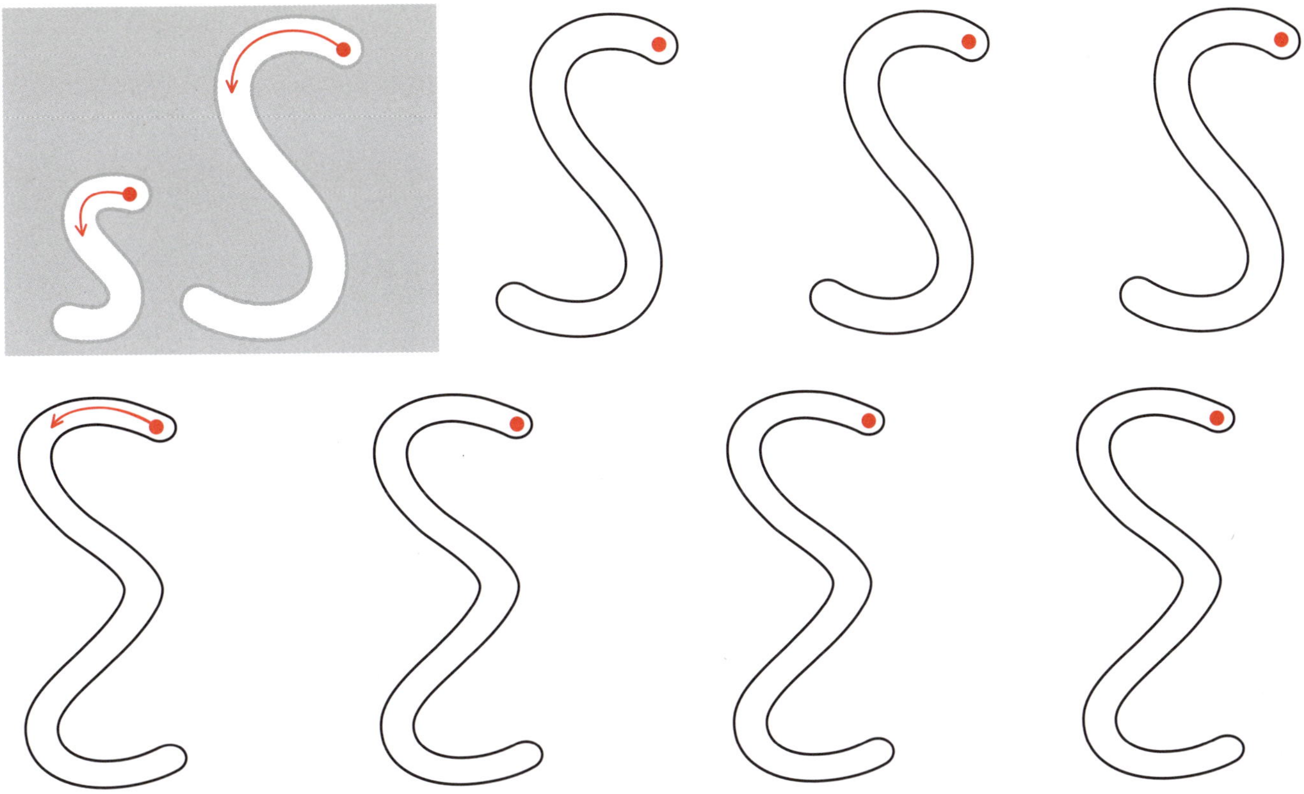

splash

get.ga/PMWA43

Trace the letter.

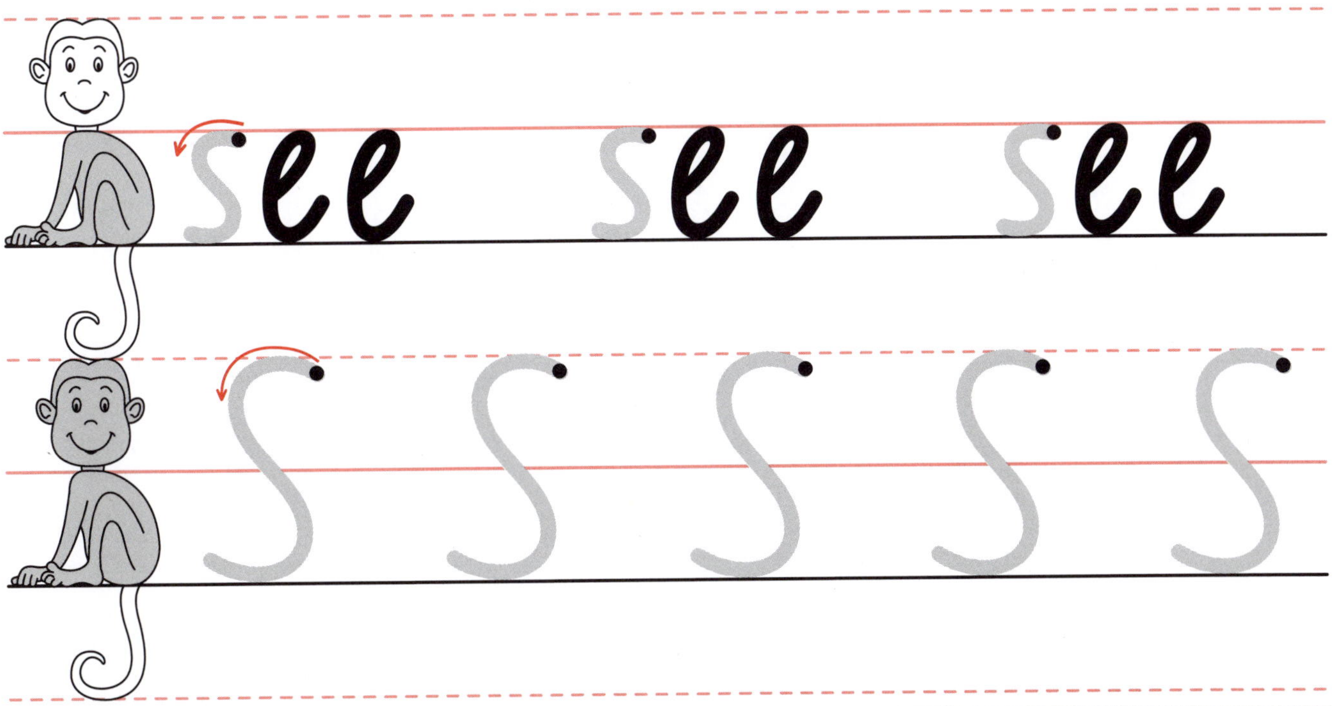

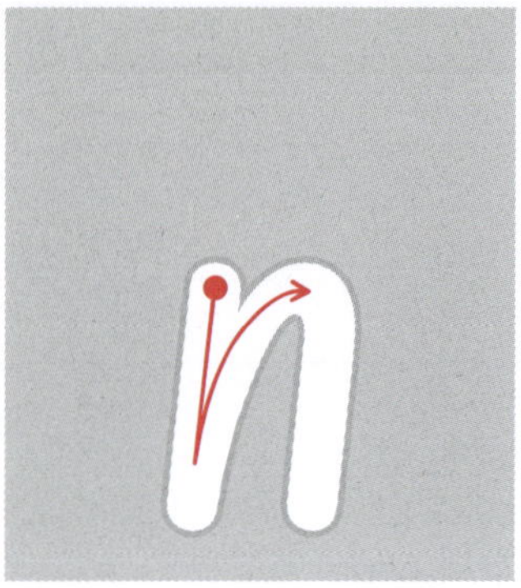

nose

Start at the dot. Follow the arrow.

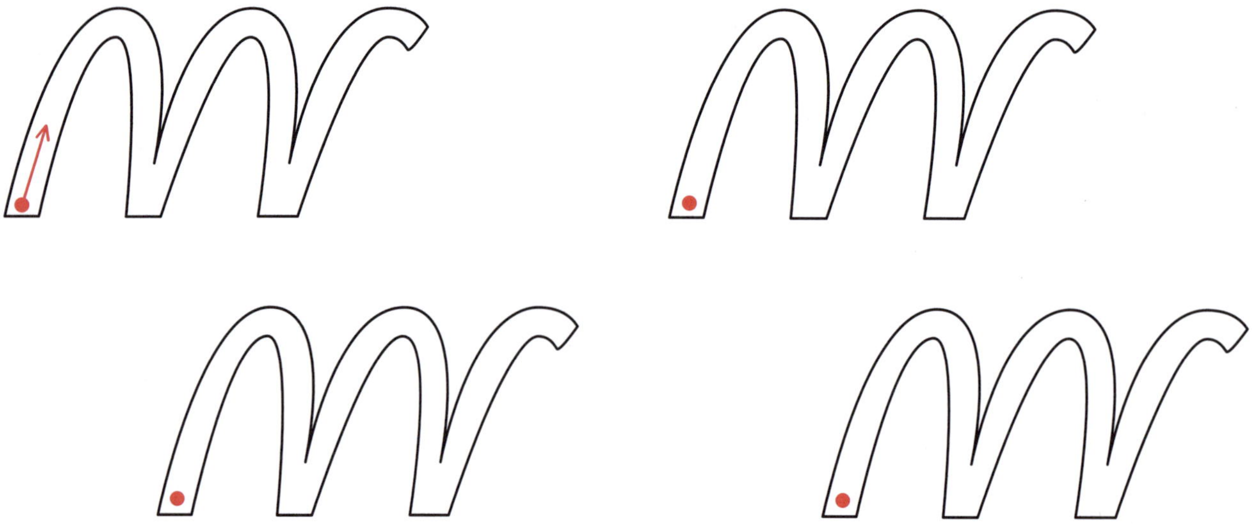

nest

1 2

n N

N N N

m m m

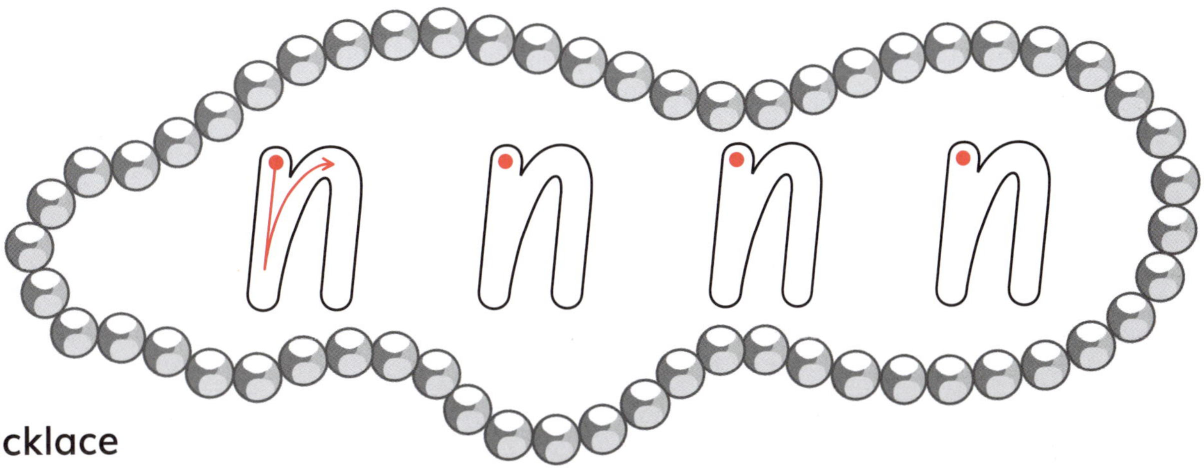

necklace

Trace the letter.

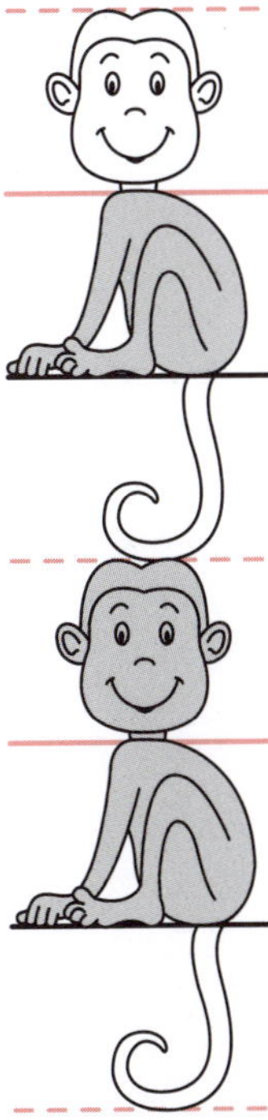

now now now

N N N N N

ISBN: 9780170416887

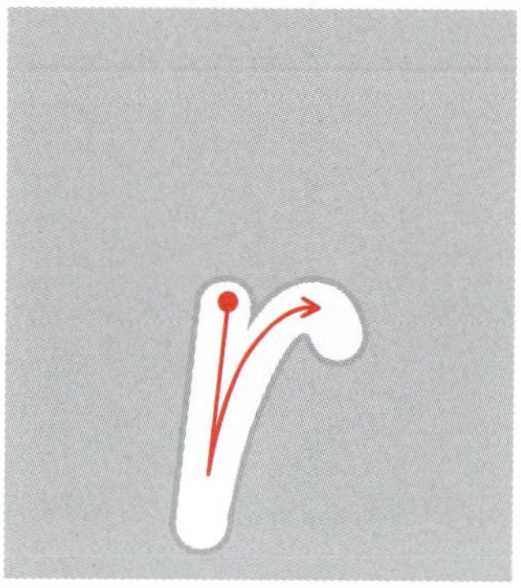

rain

Start at the dot. Follow the arrow.

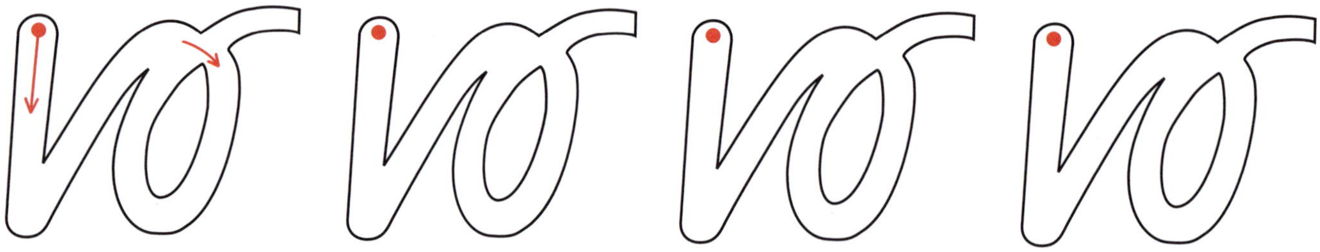

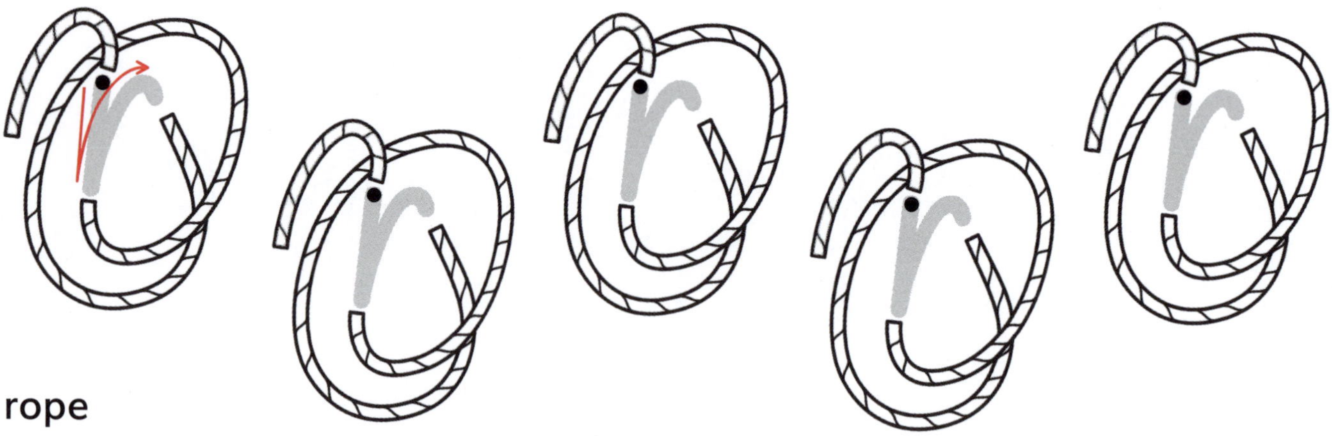

rope

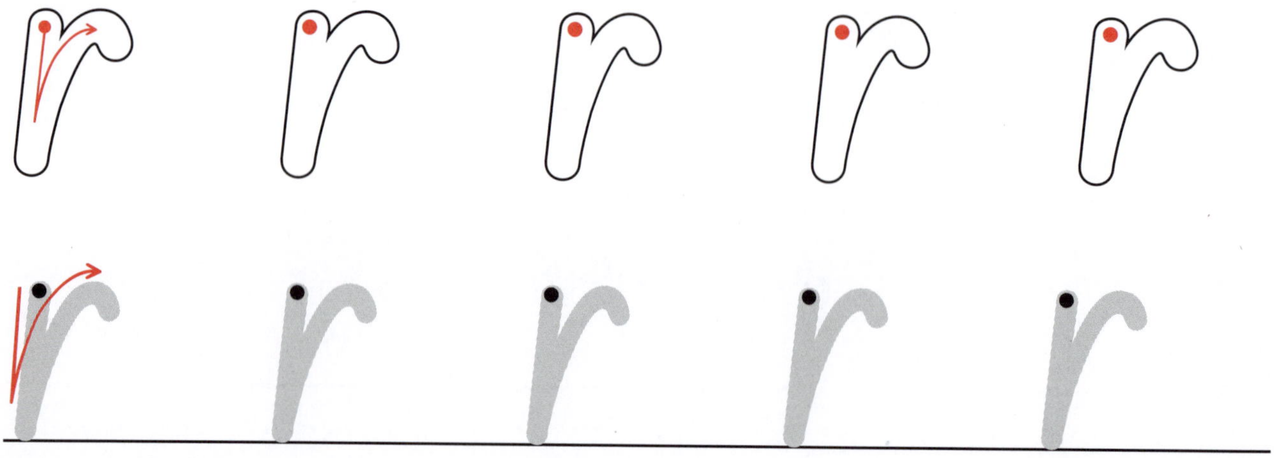

ISBN: 9780170416887

robot

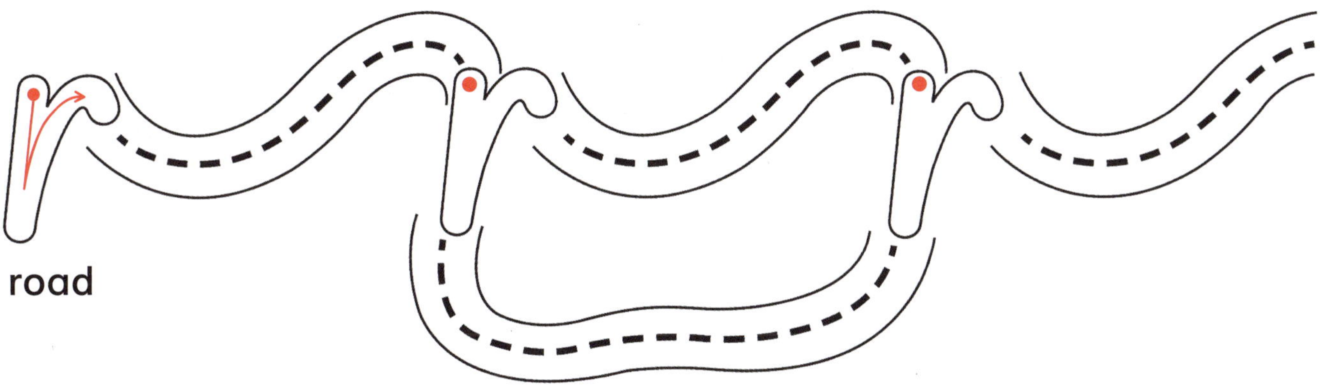

road

Trace the letter.

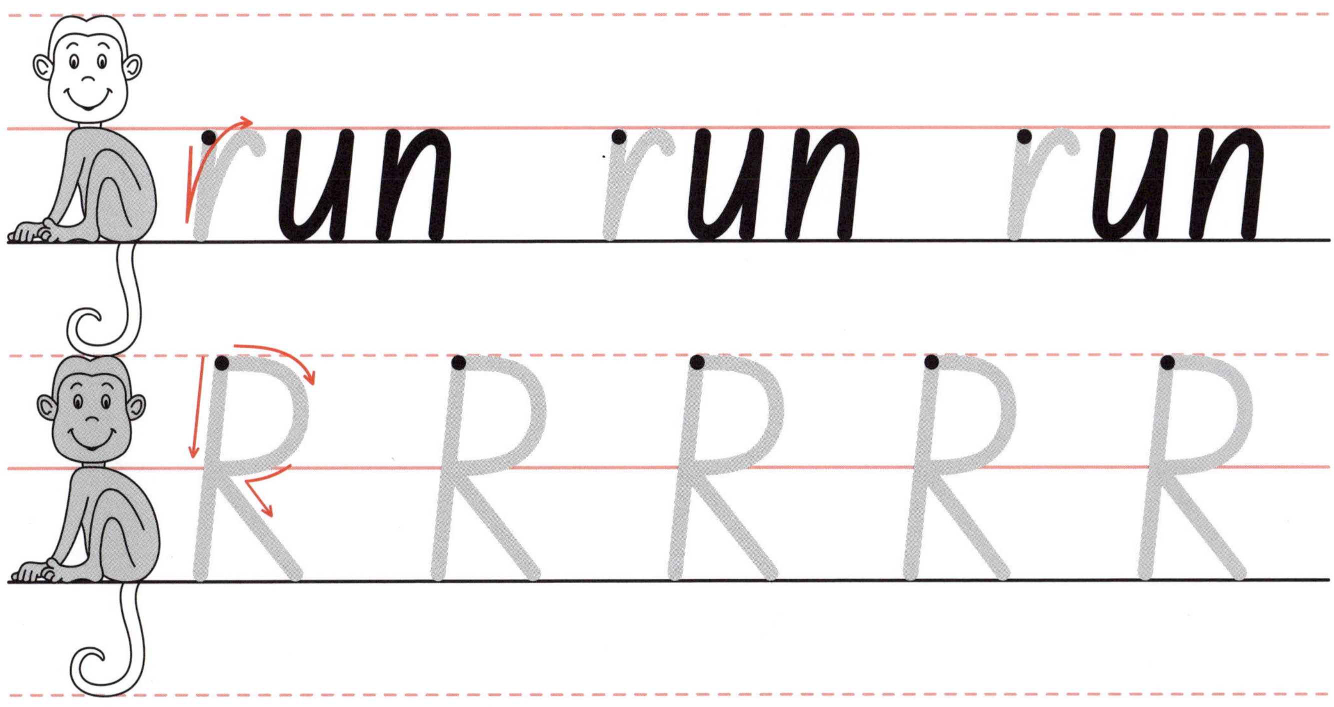

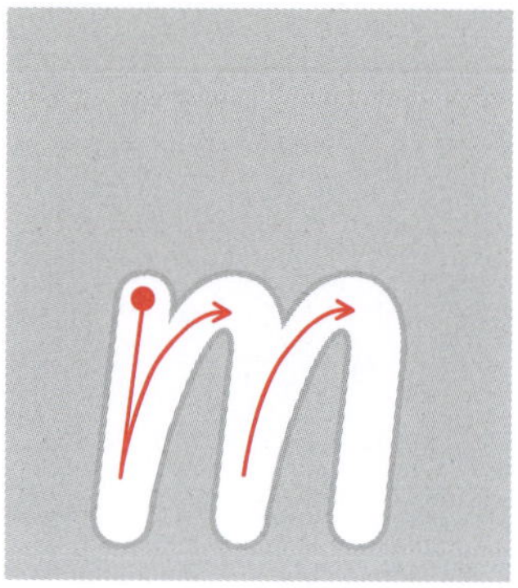

mouse

Start at the dot. Follow the arrow.

mouse

moon

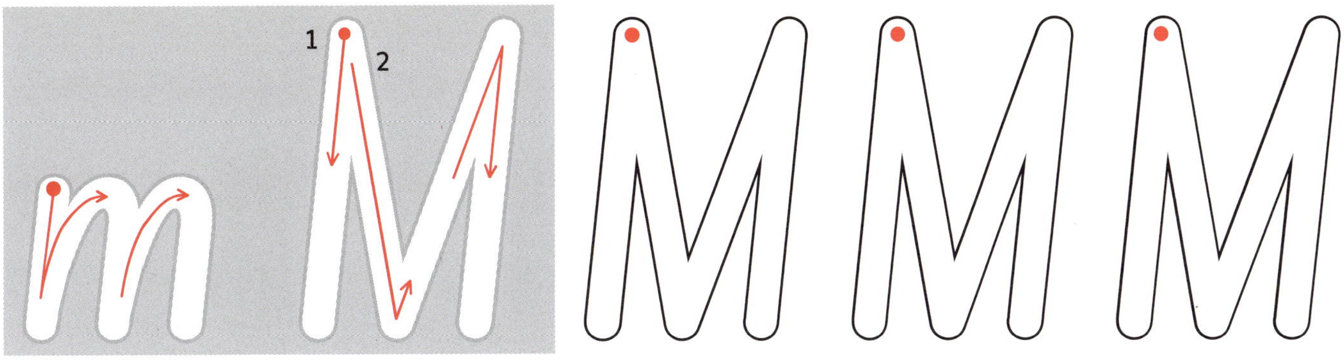

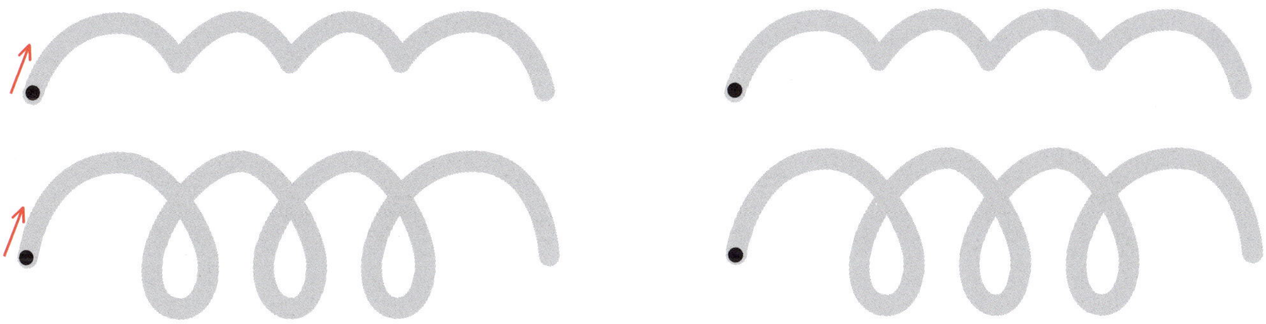

mountains

Trace the letter.

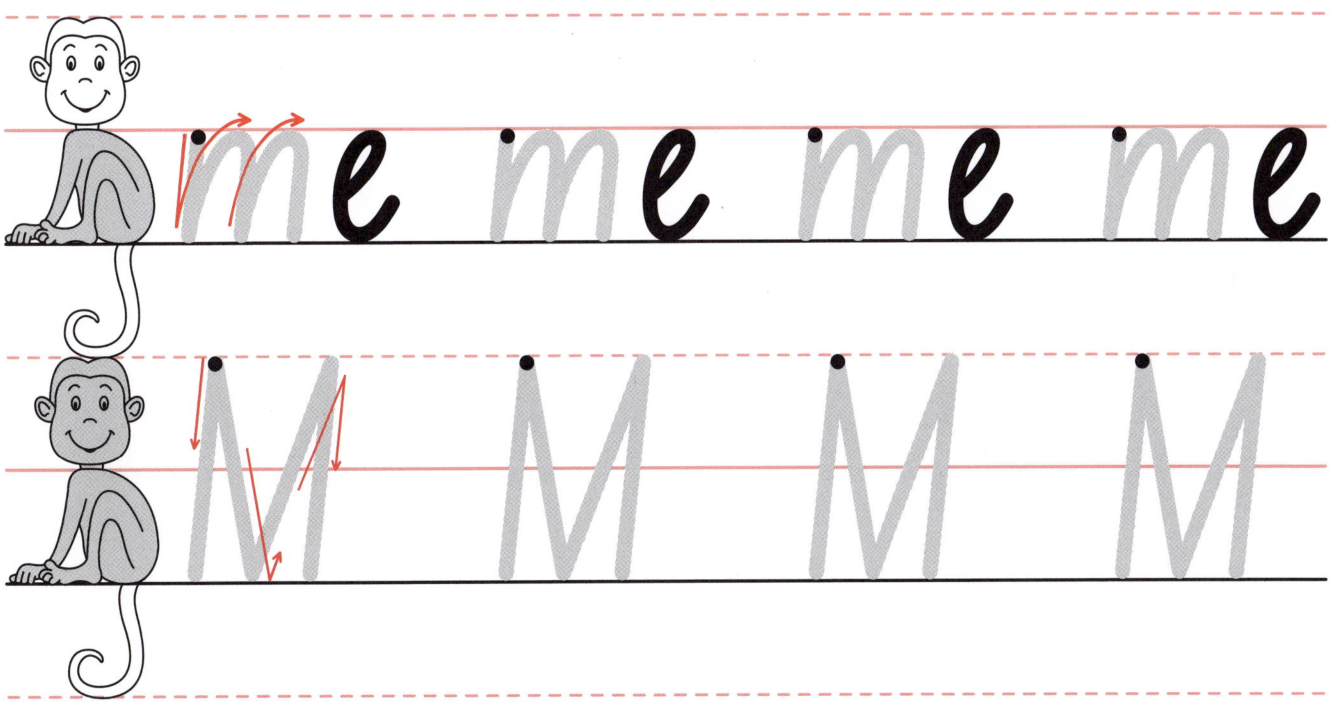

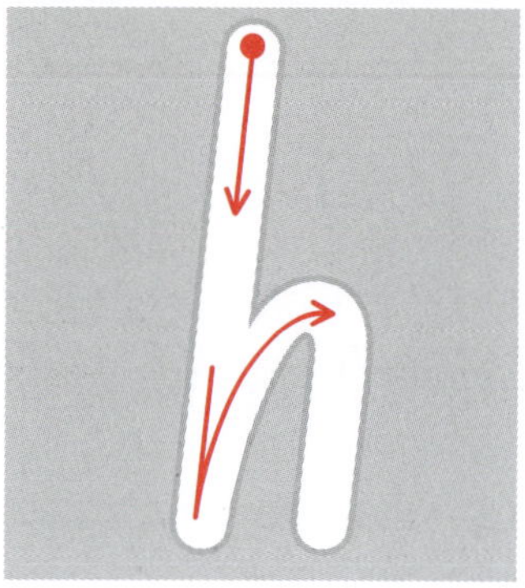

house

Start at the dot. Follow the arrow.

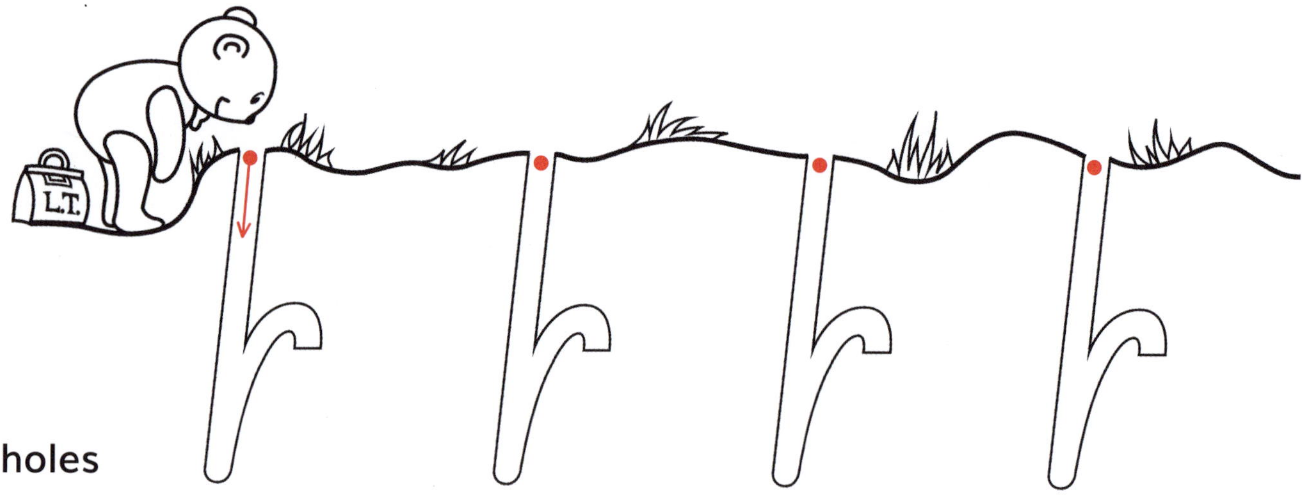

holes

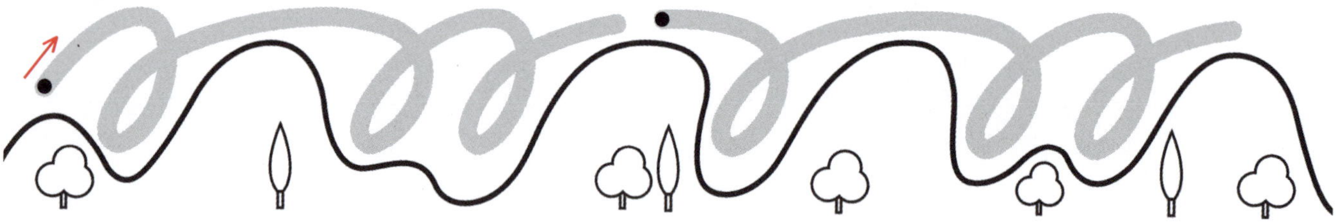

hills

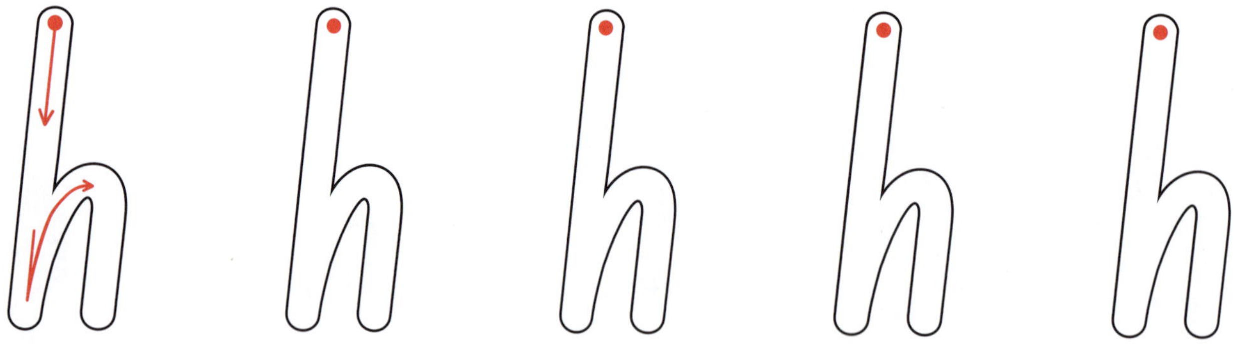

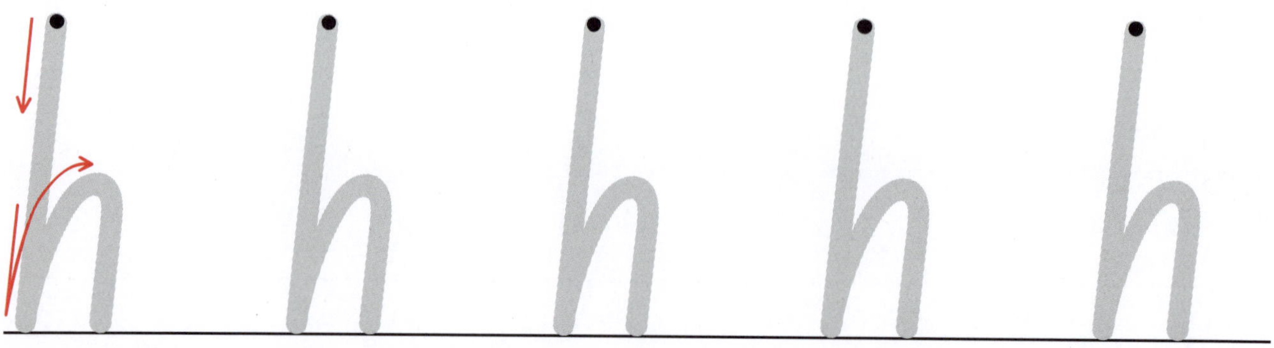

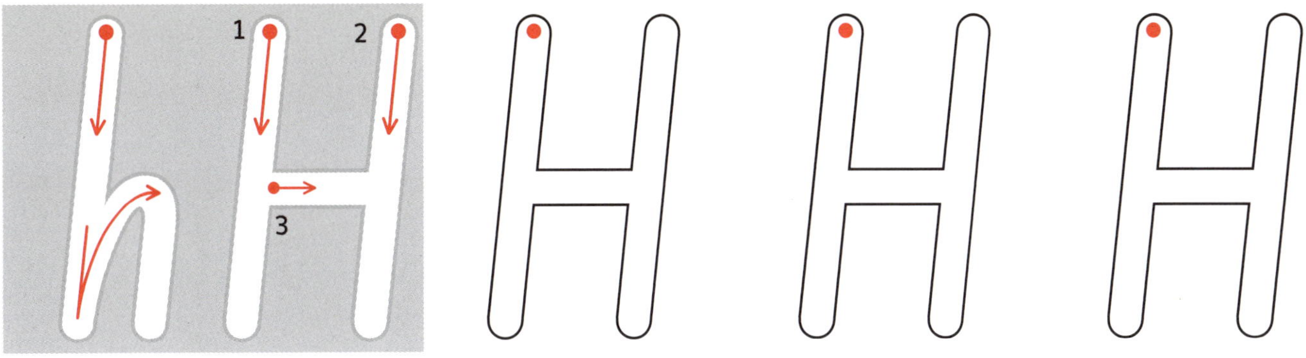

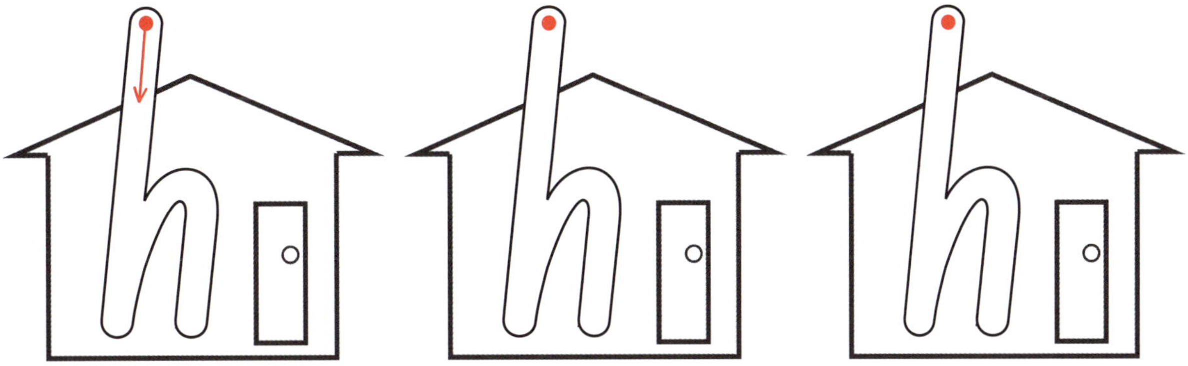

house

hat

get.ga/PMWA44

Trace the letter.

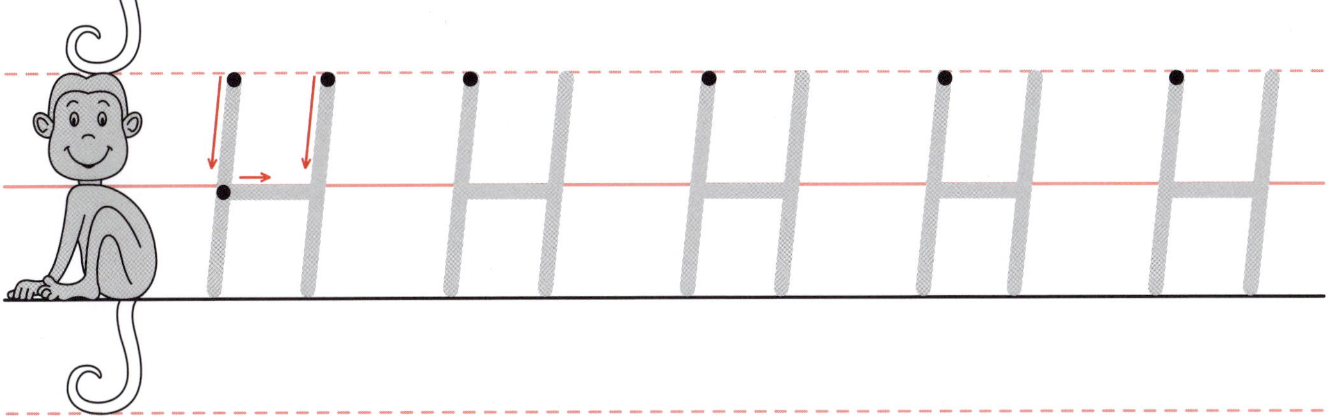

ISBN: 9780170416887

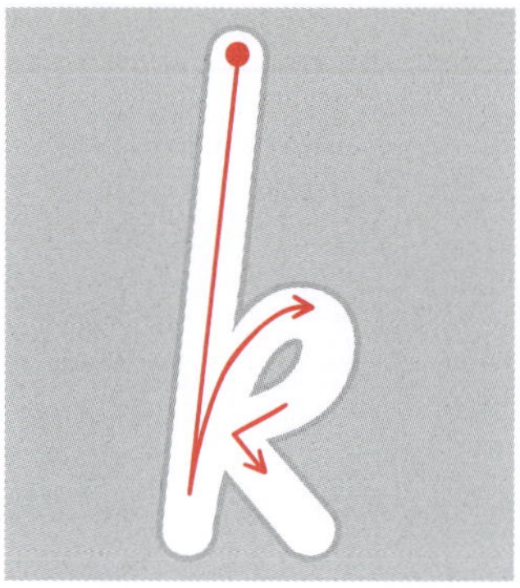

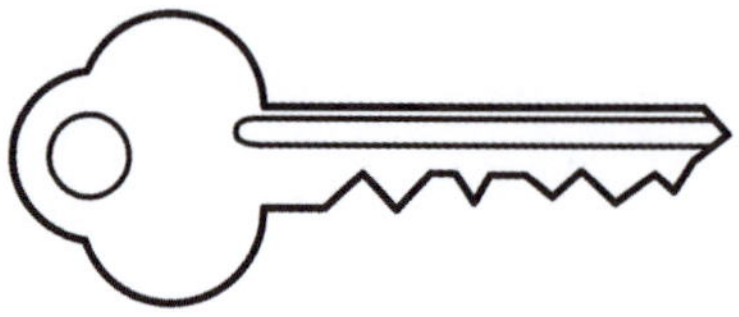

key

Start at the dot. Follow the arrow.

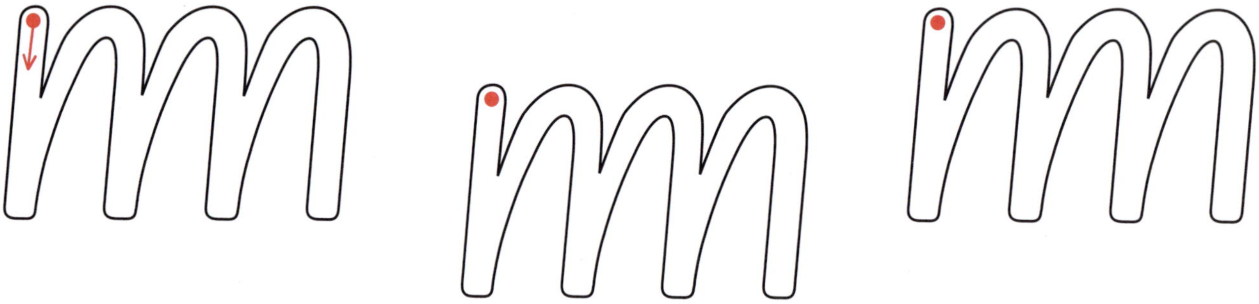

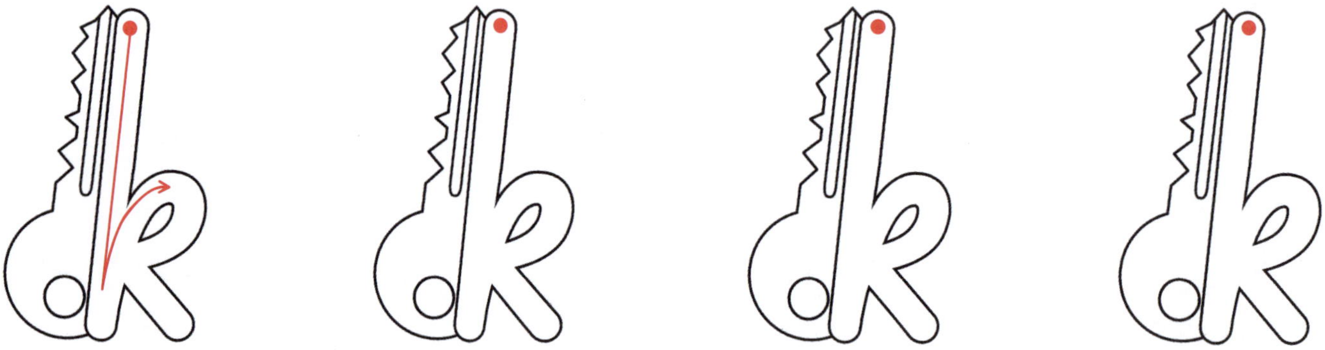

key

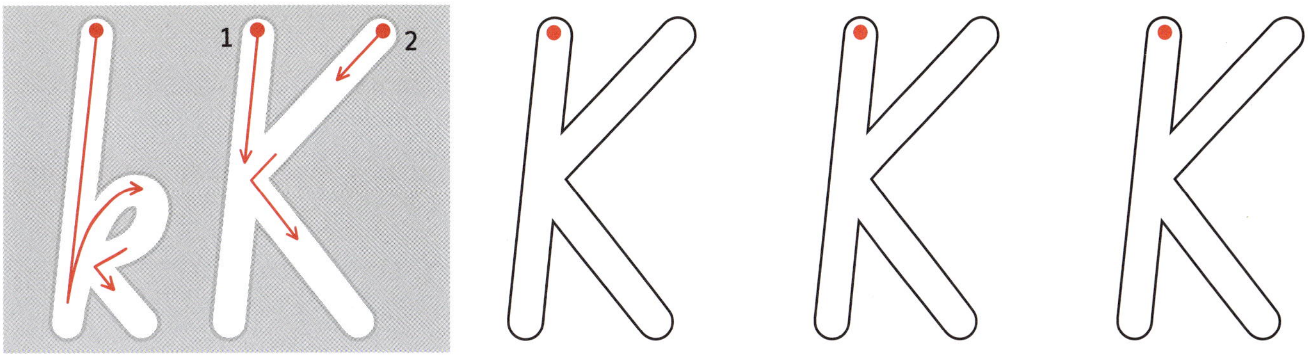

kangaroo

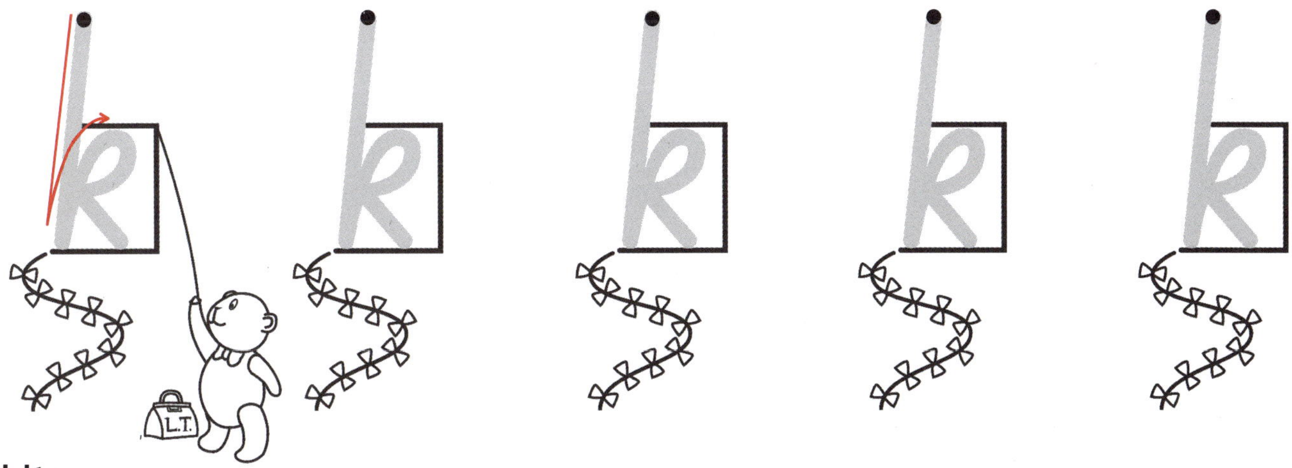

kite

Trace the letter.

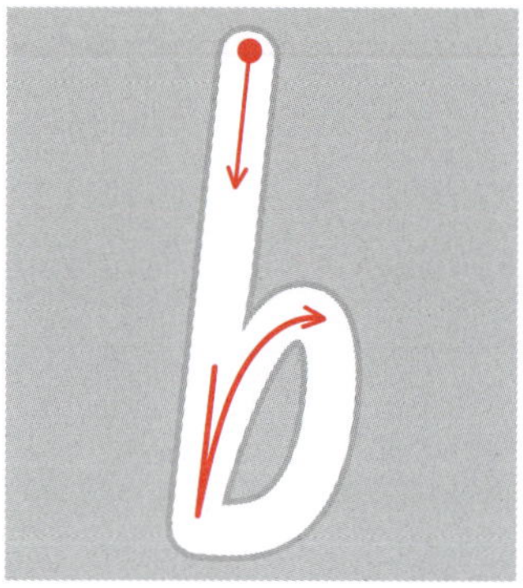

balloons

Start at the dot. Follow the arrow.

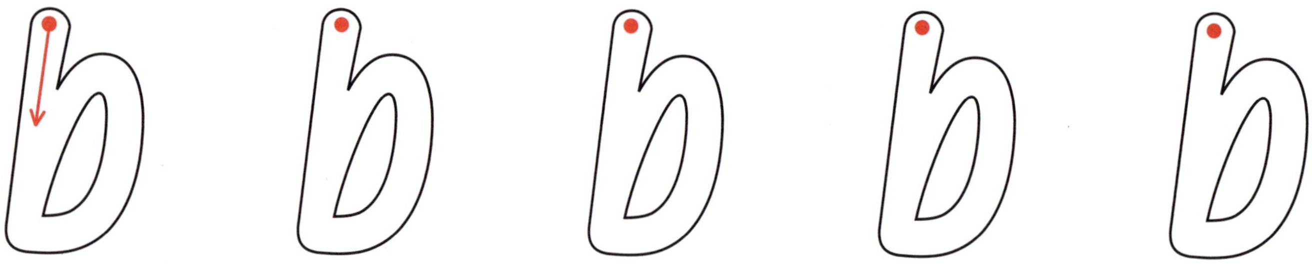

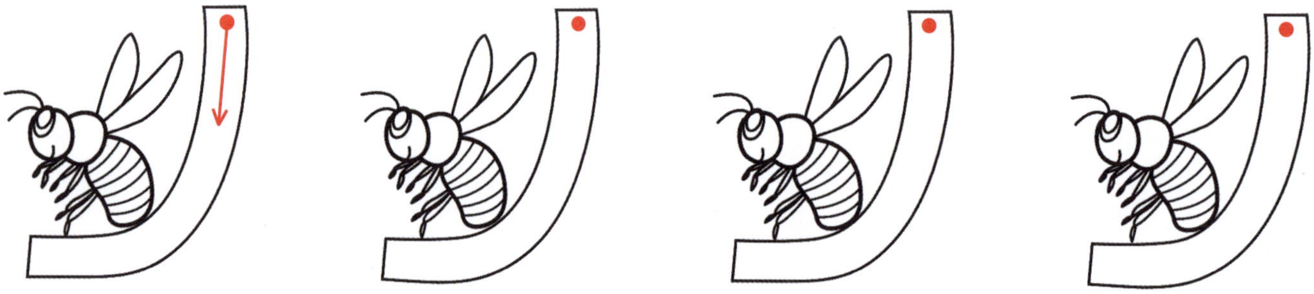

bee

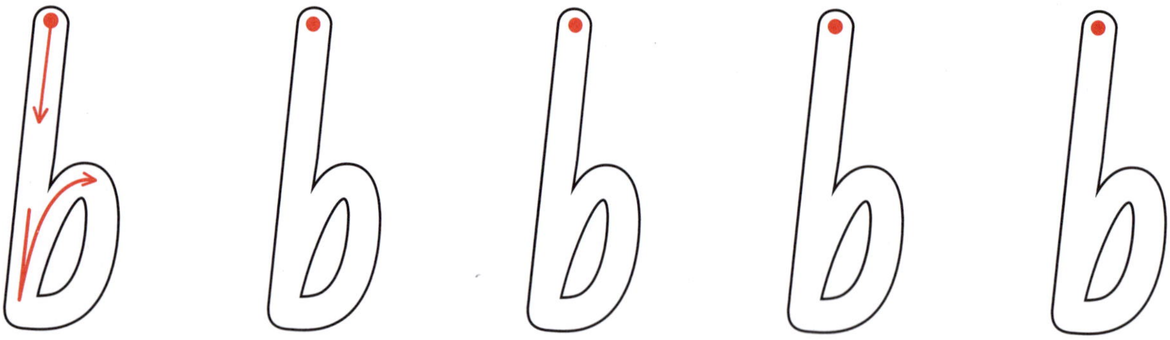

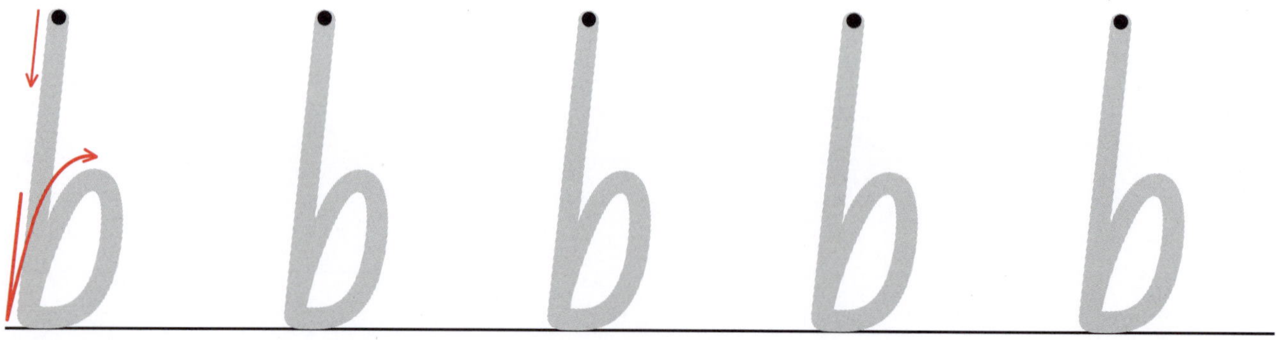

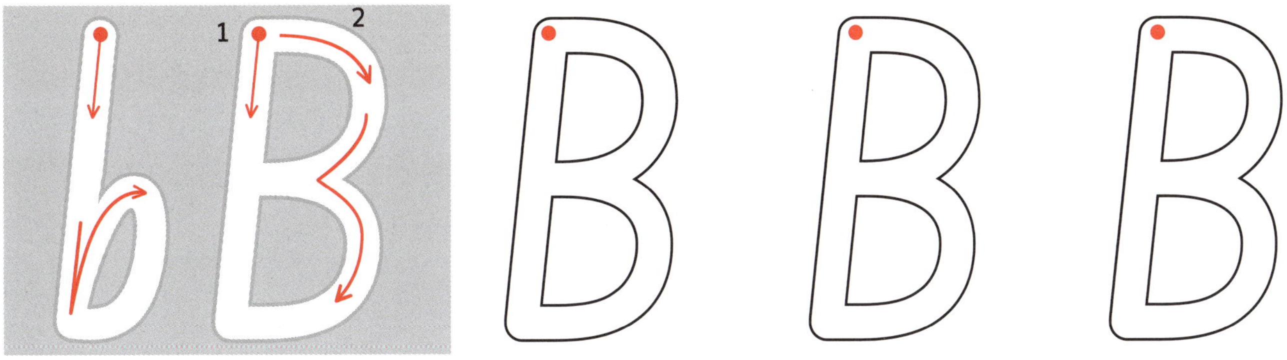

boat

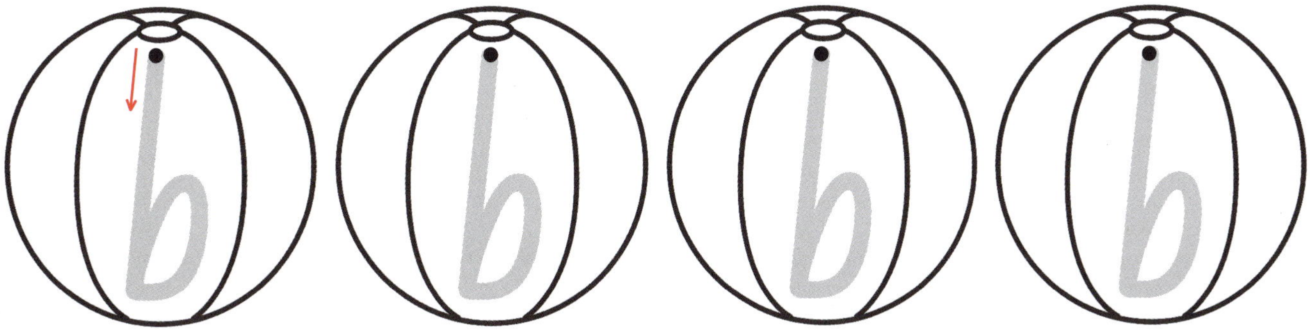

ball

Trace the letter.

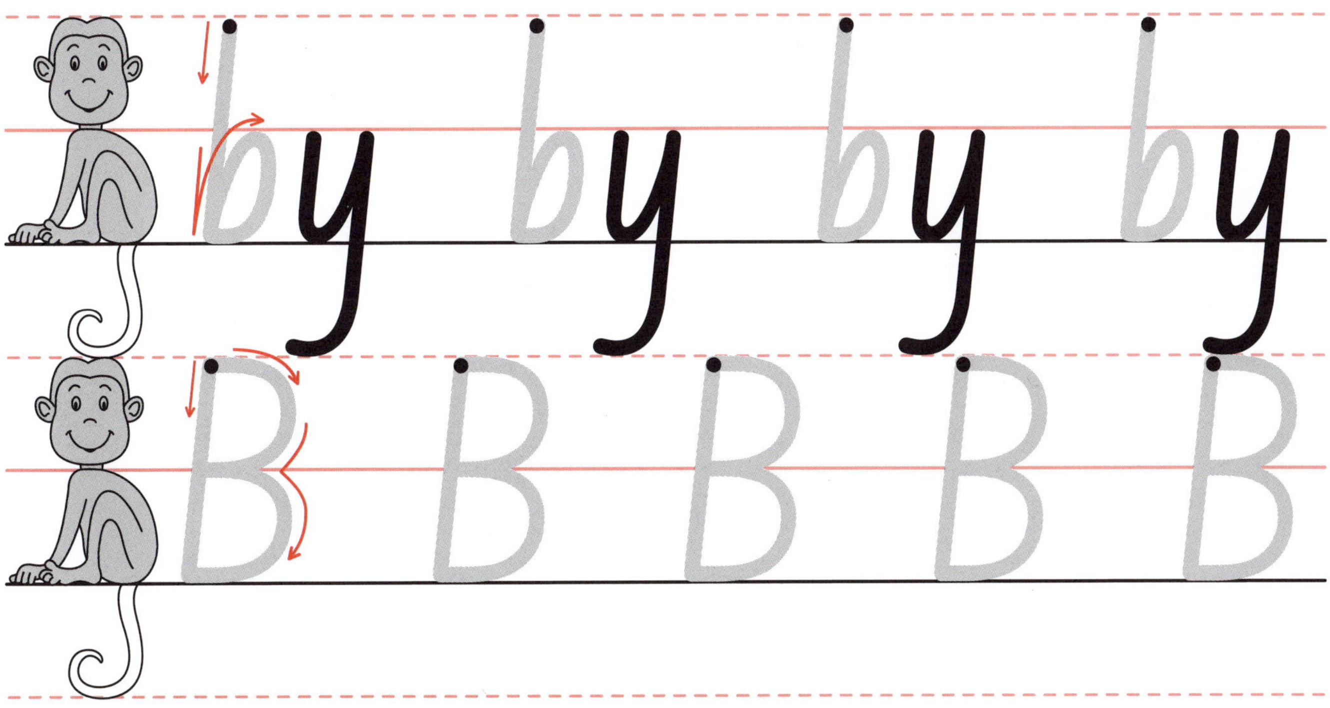

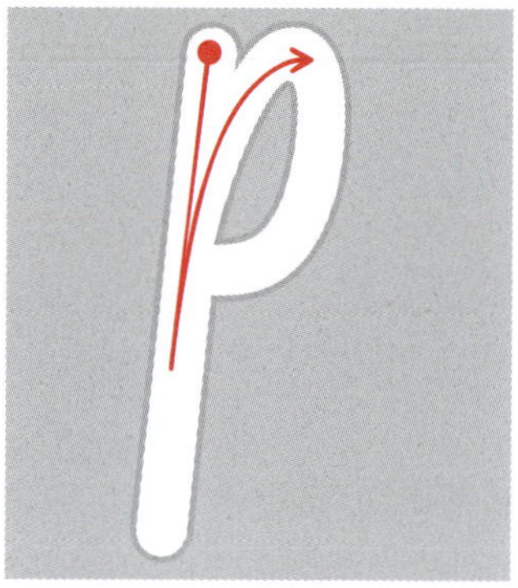

paint

Start at the dot. Follow the arrow.

pencil

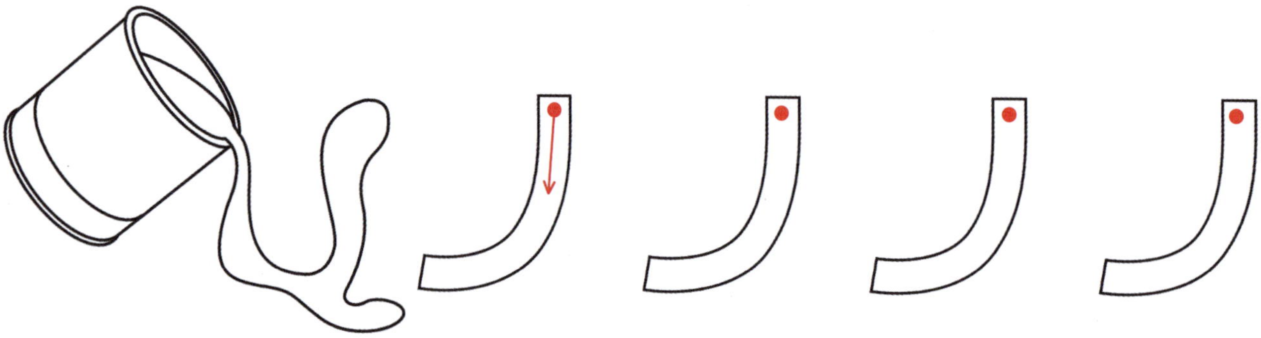

paint

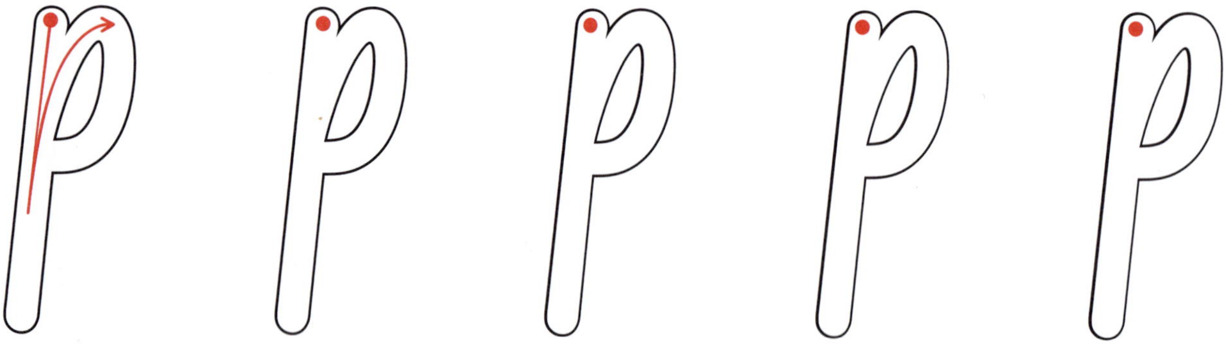

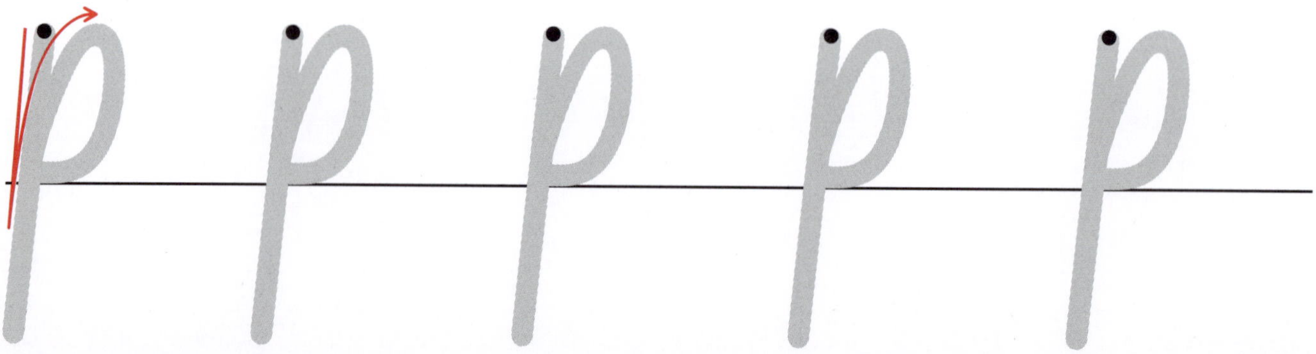

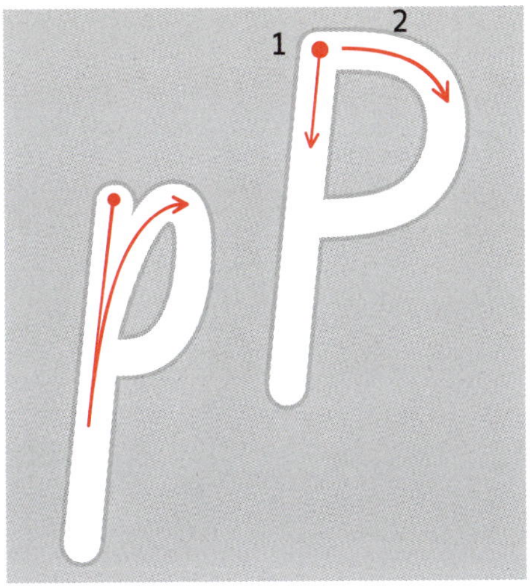

puppy

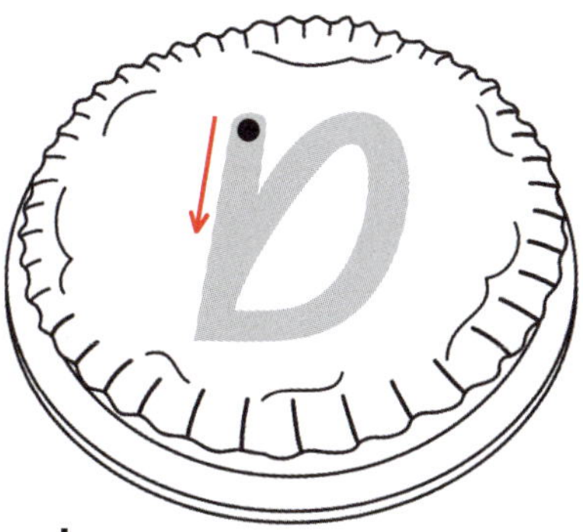

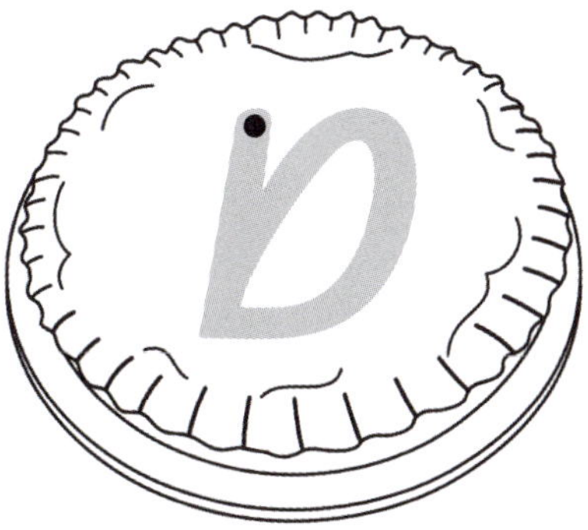

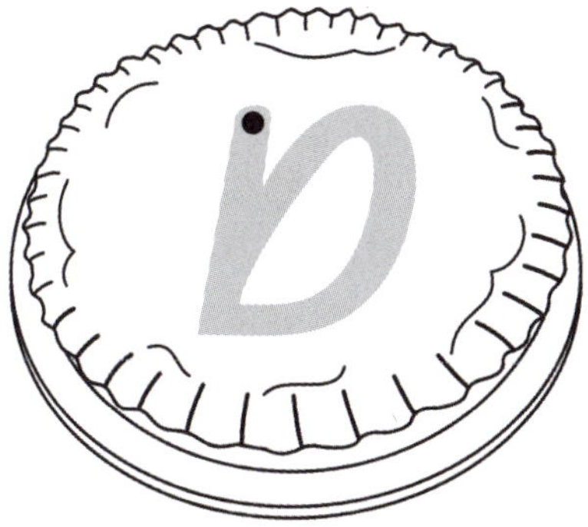

pie

Trace the letter.

get.ga/PMWA45

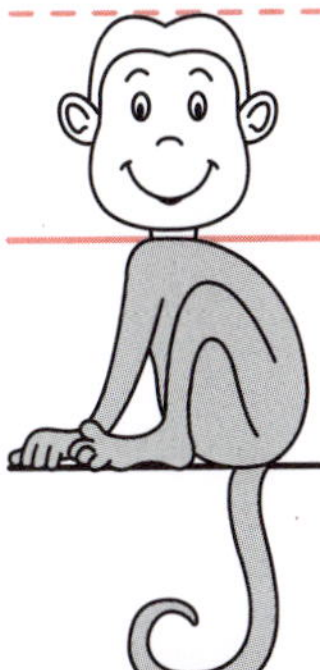

play play play

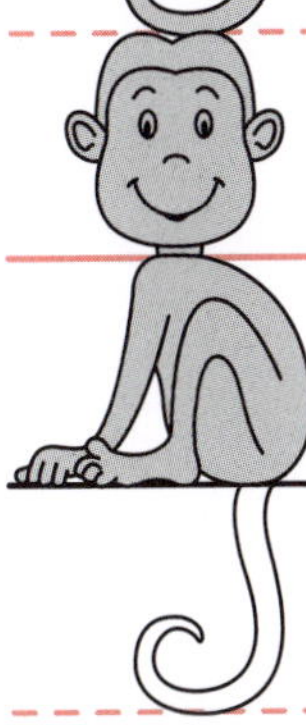

P P P P P

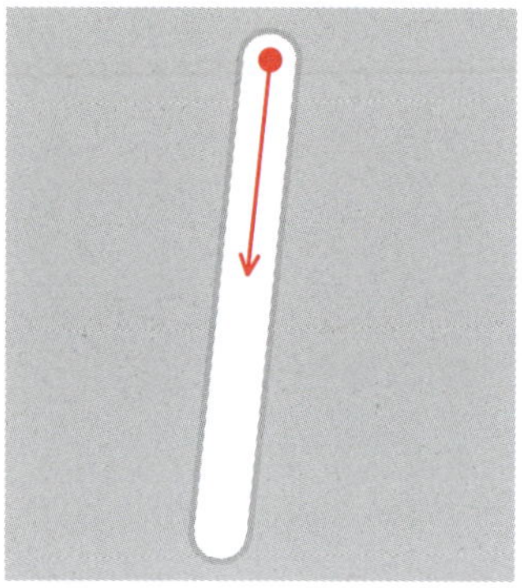

ladder

Start at the dot. Follow the arrow.

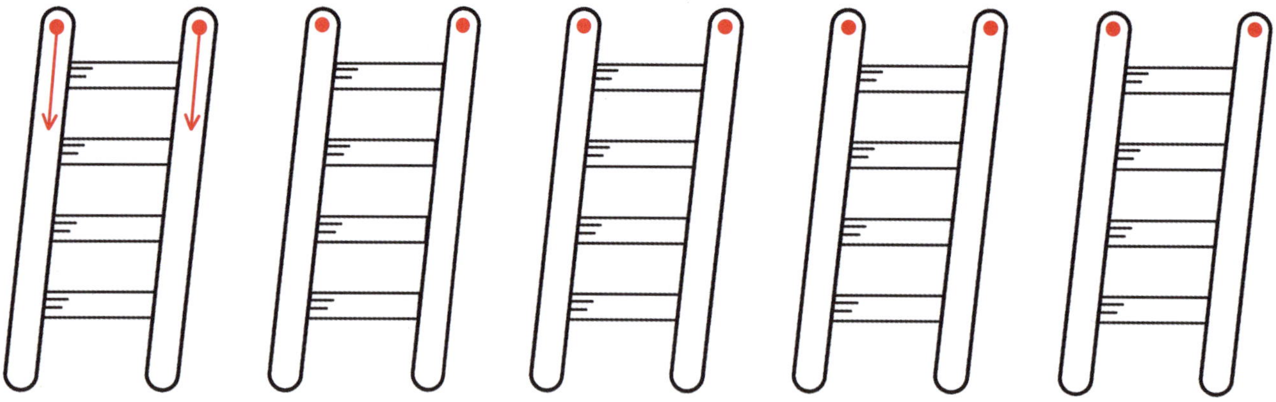

ladder

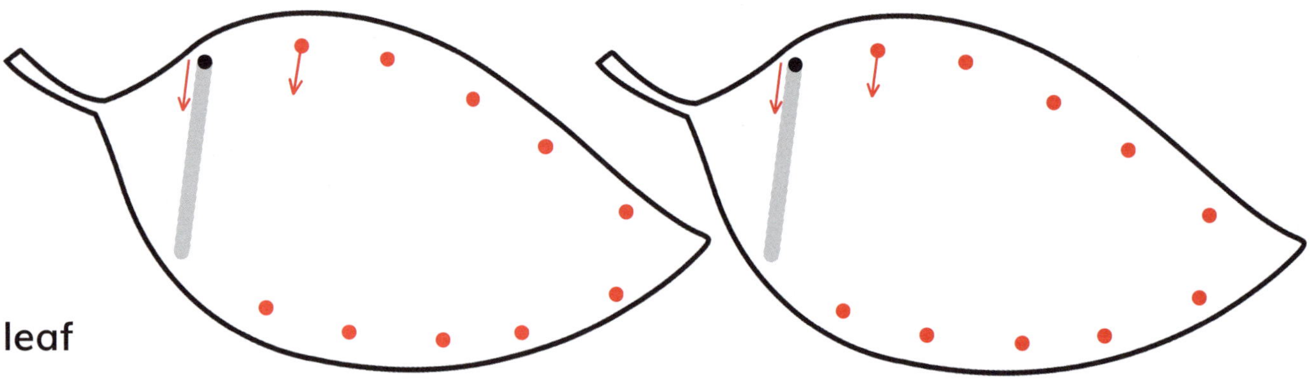

leaf

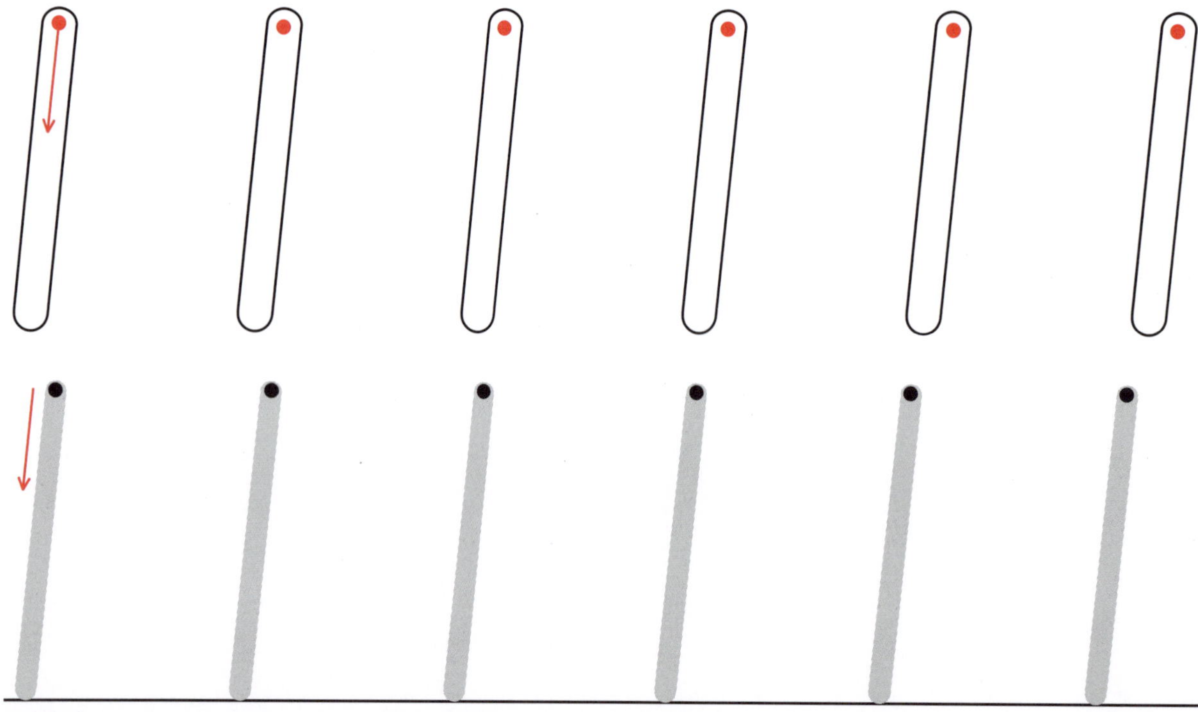

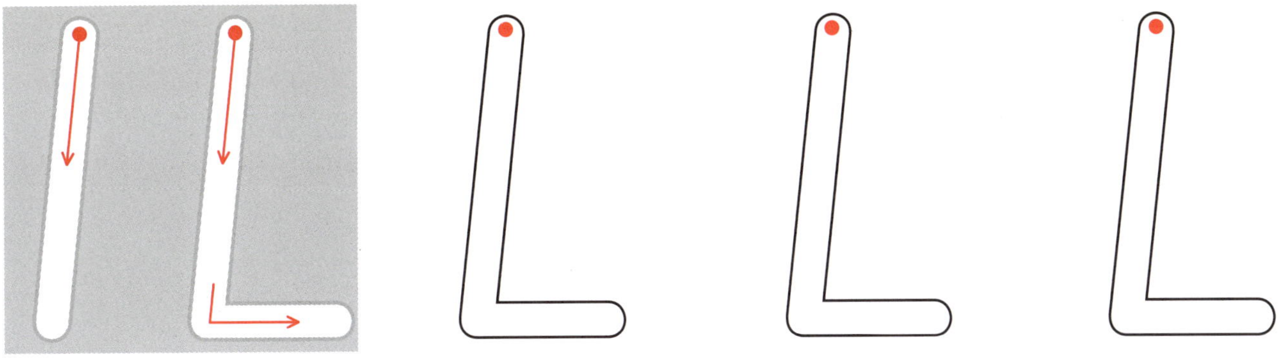

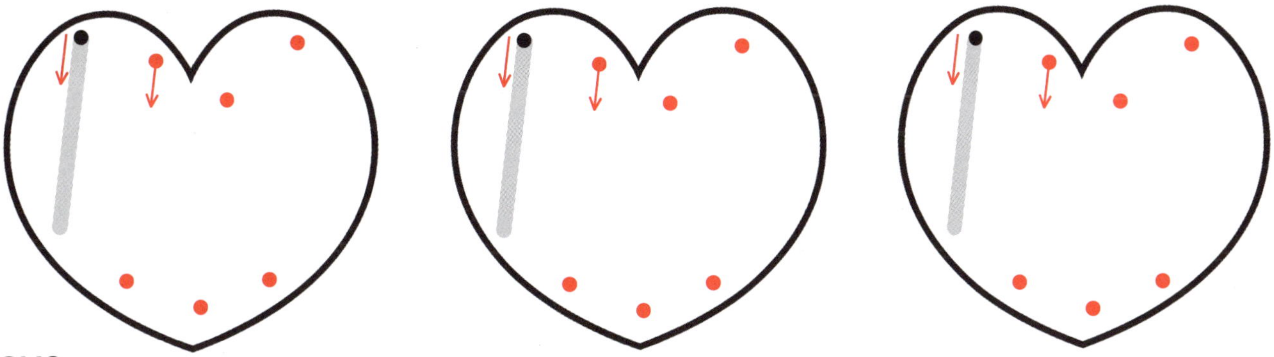

love

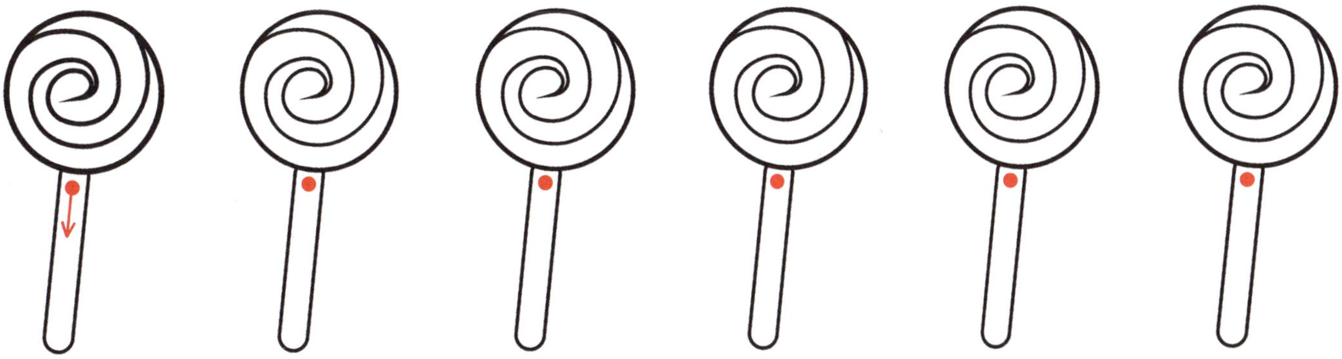

lollipop

Trace the letter.

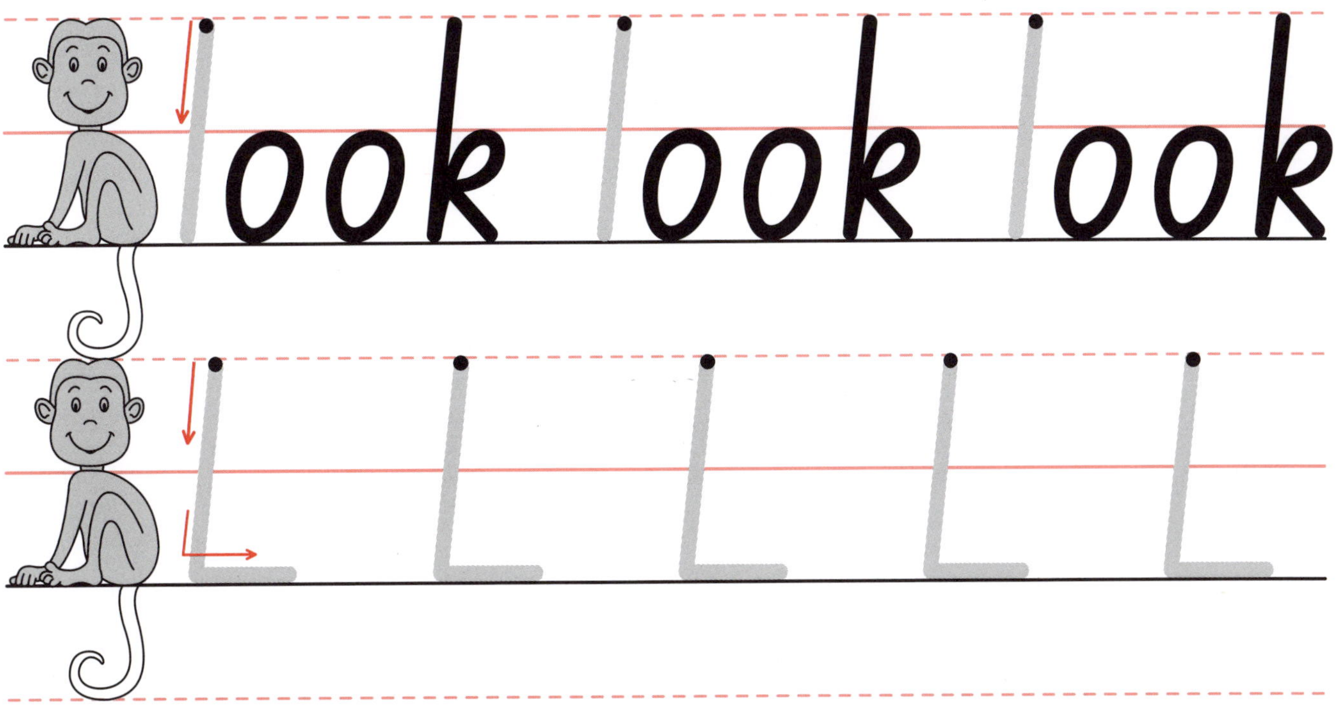

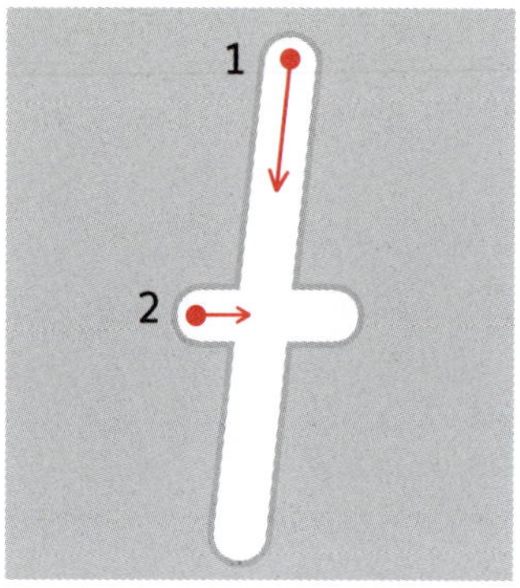

tree

Start at the dot. Follow the arrow.

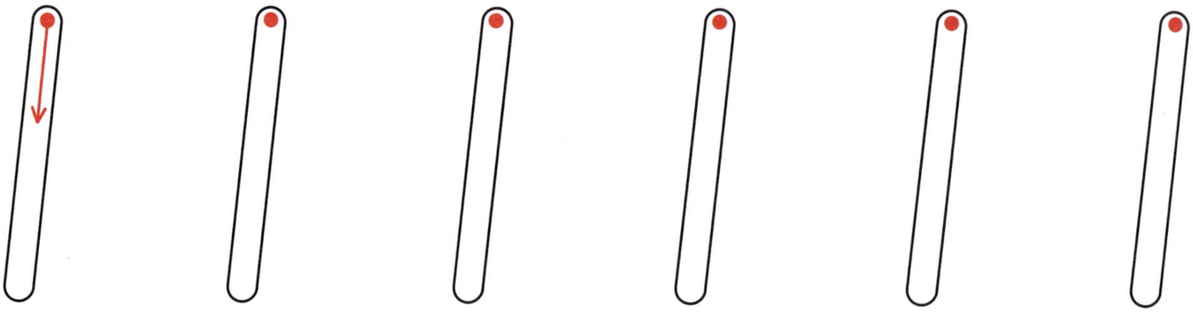

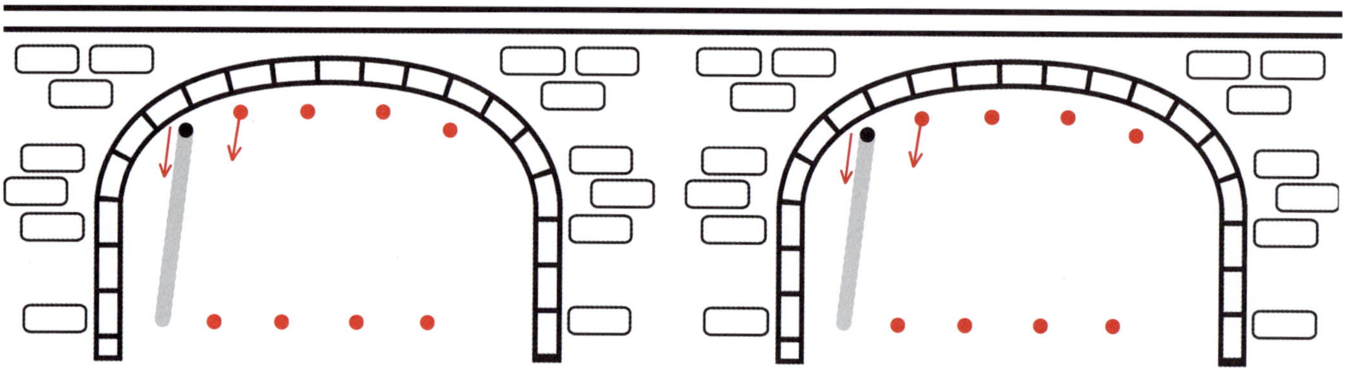

tunnels

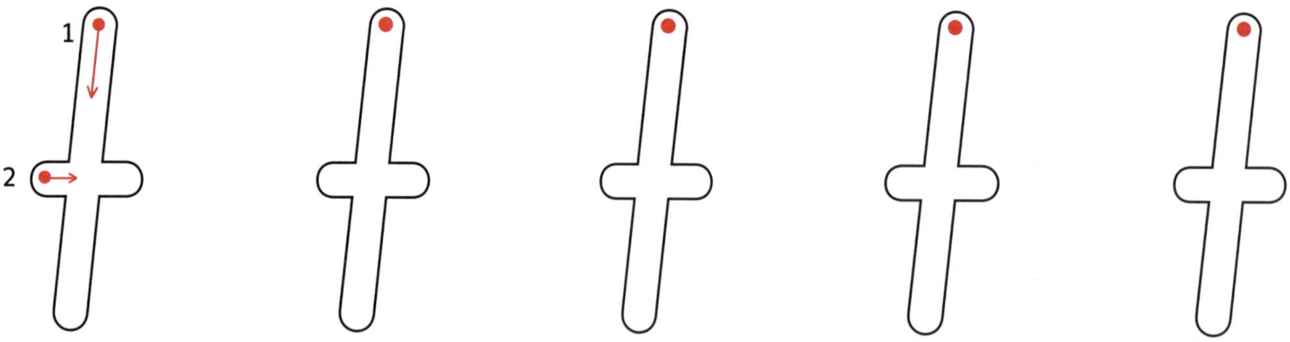

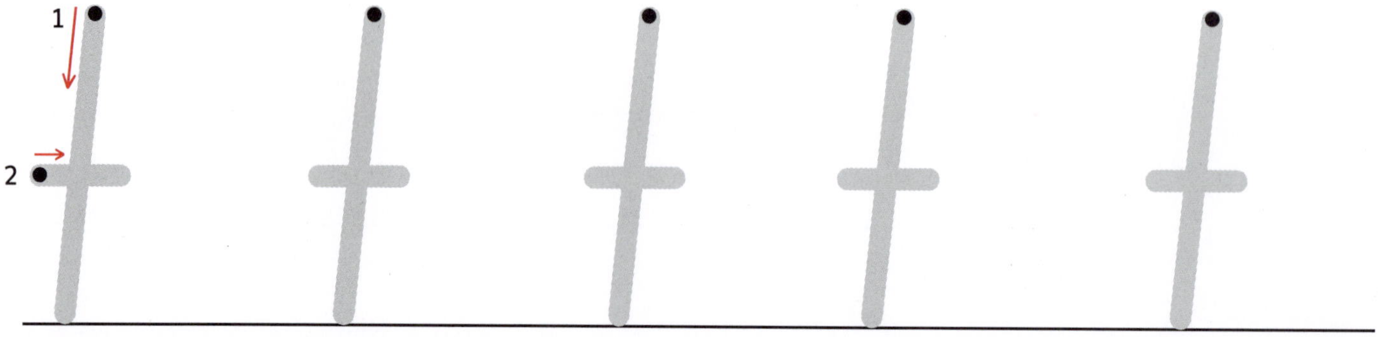

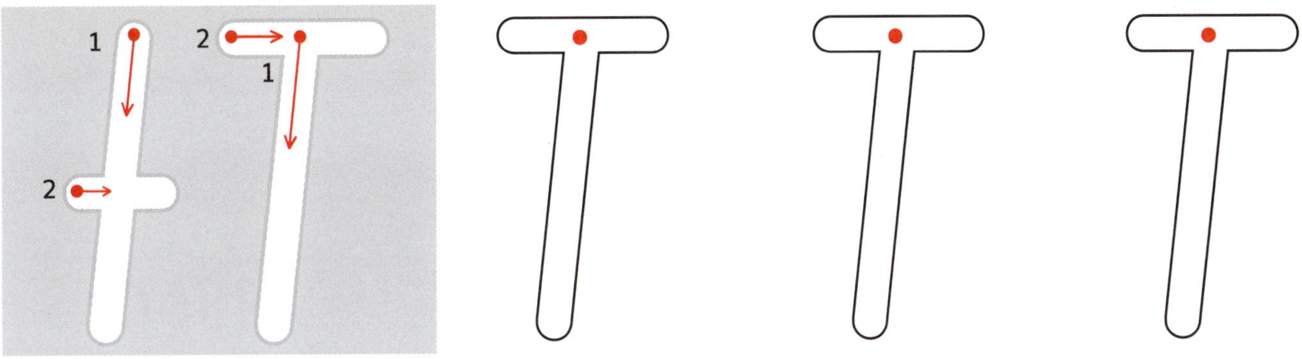

tiger

tent

Trace the letter.

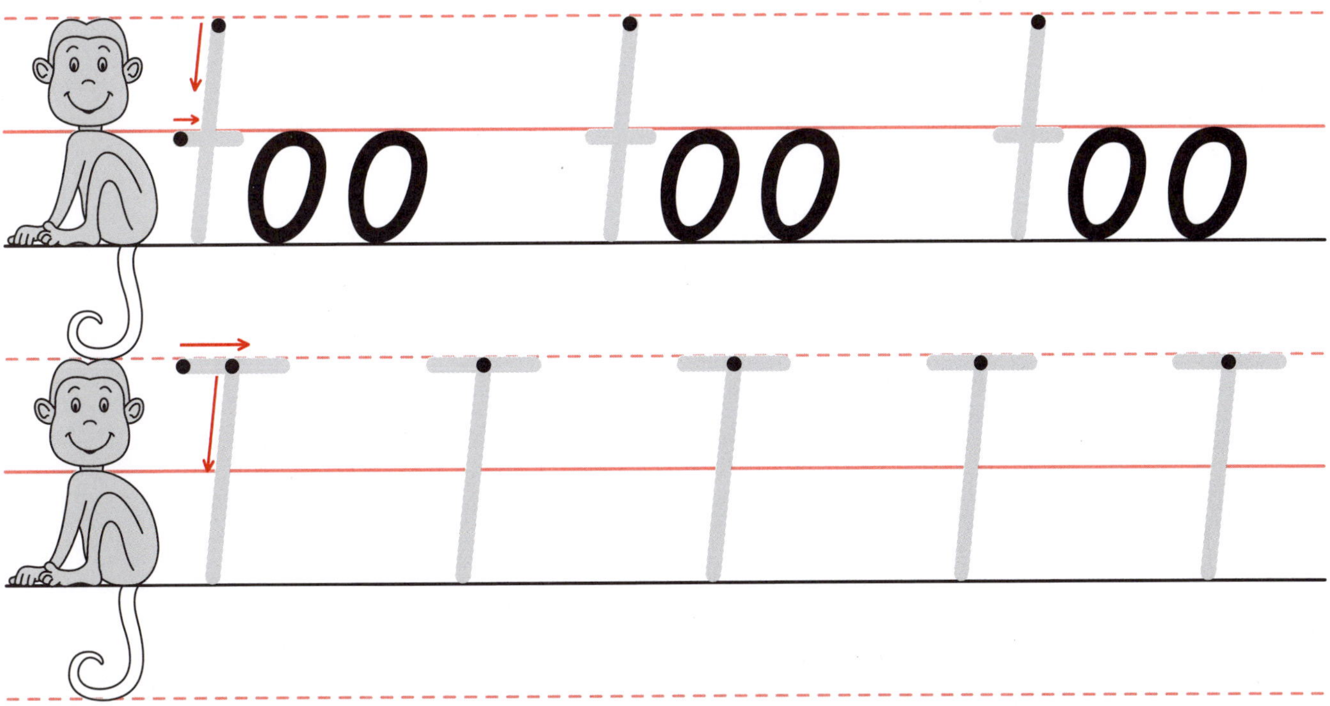

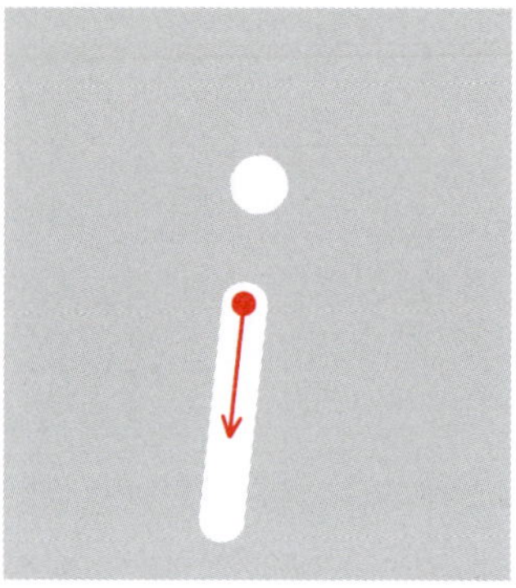

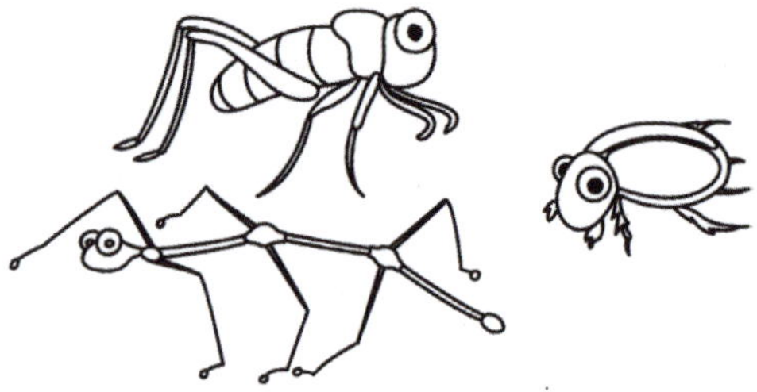

insects

Start at the dot. Follow the arrow.

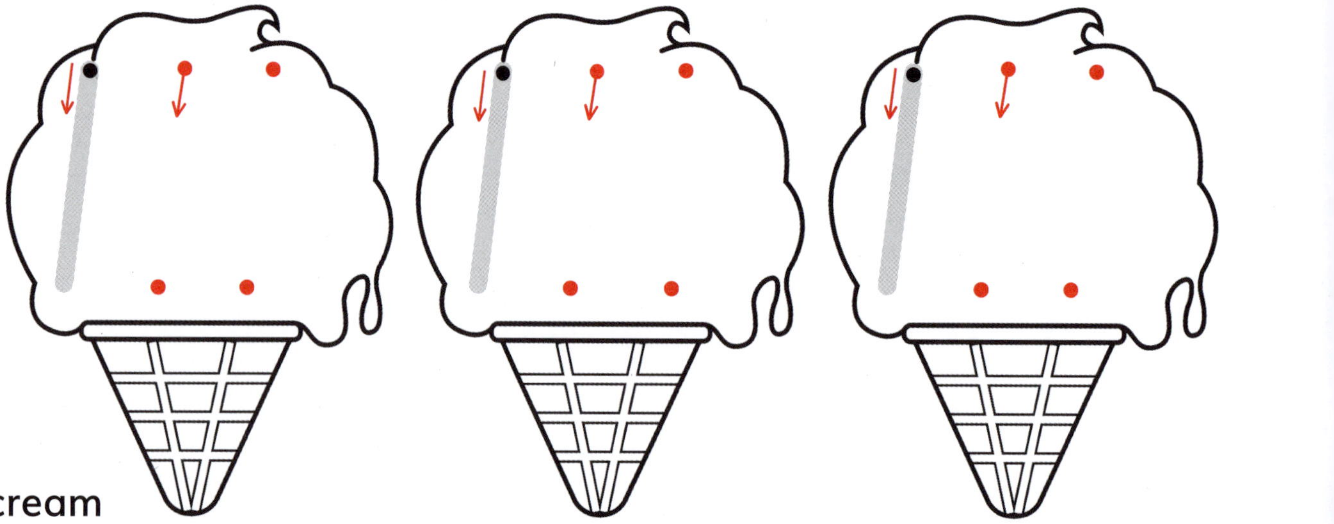

ice cream

igloo

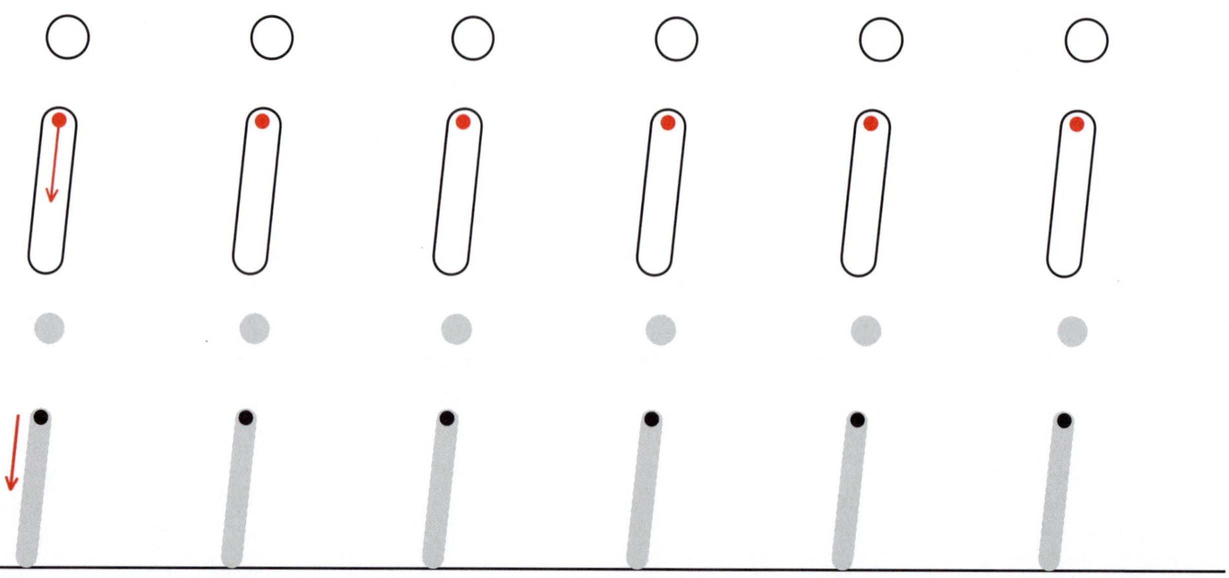

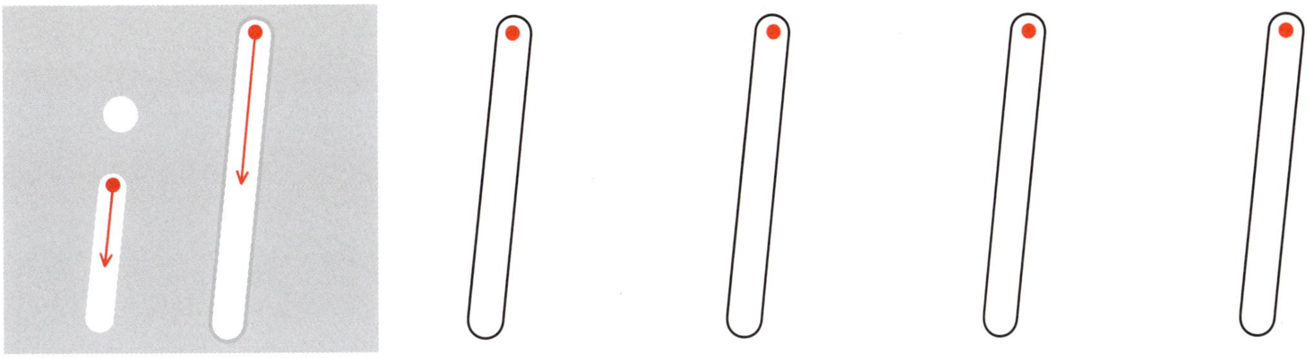

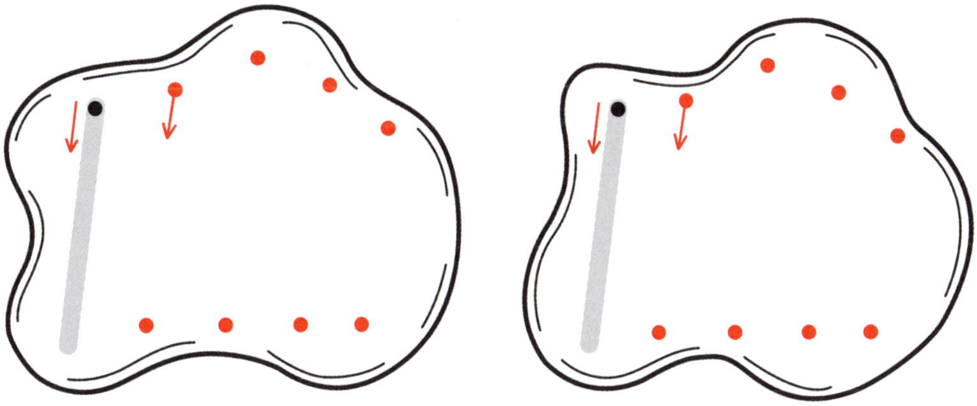

jump in

island

Trace the letter.

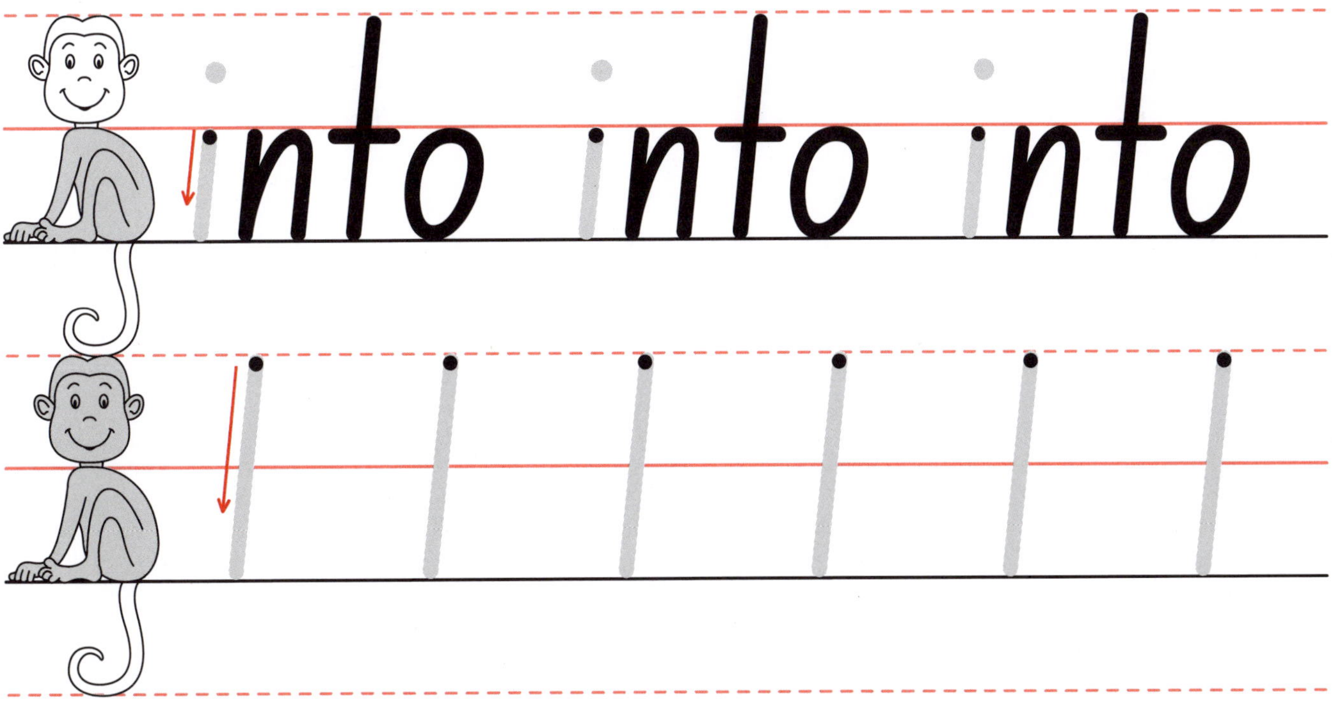

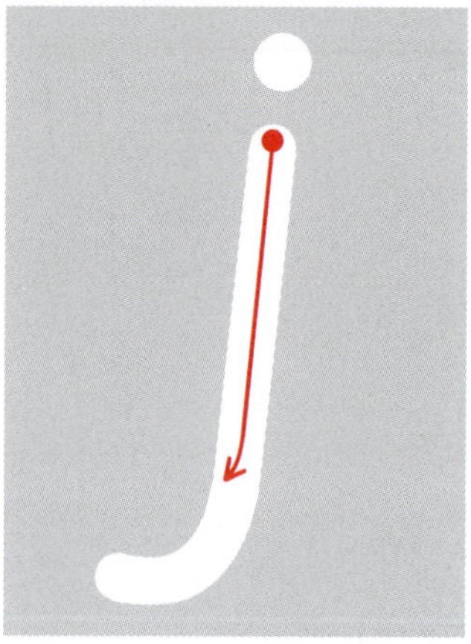

jam

Start at the dot. Follow the arrow.

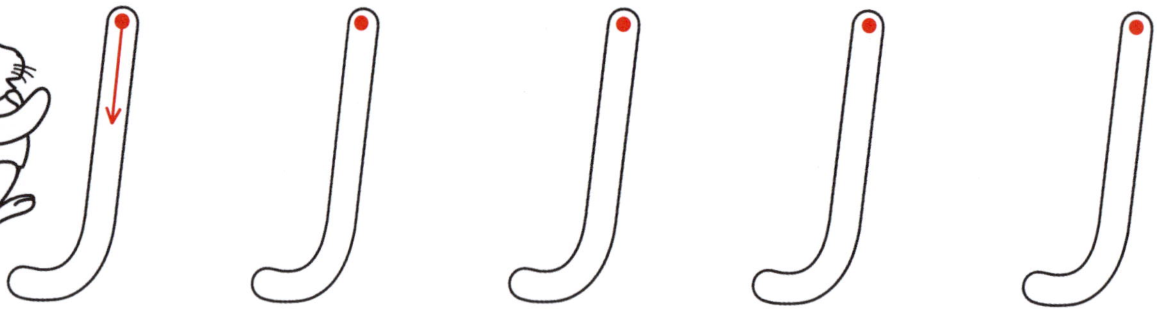

jump

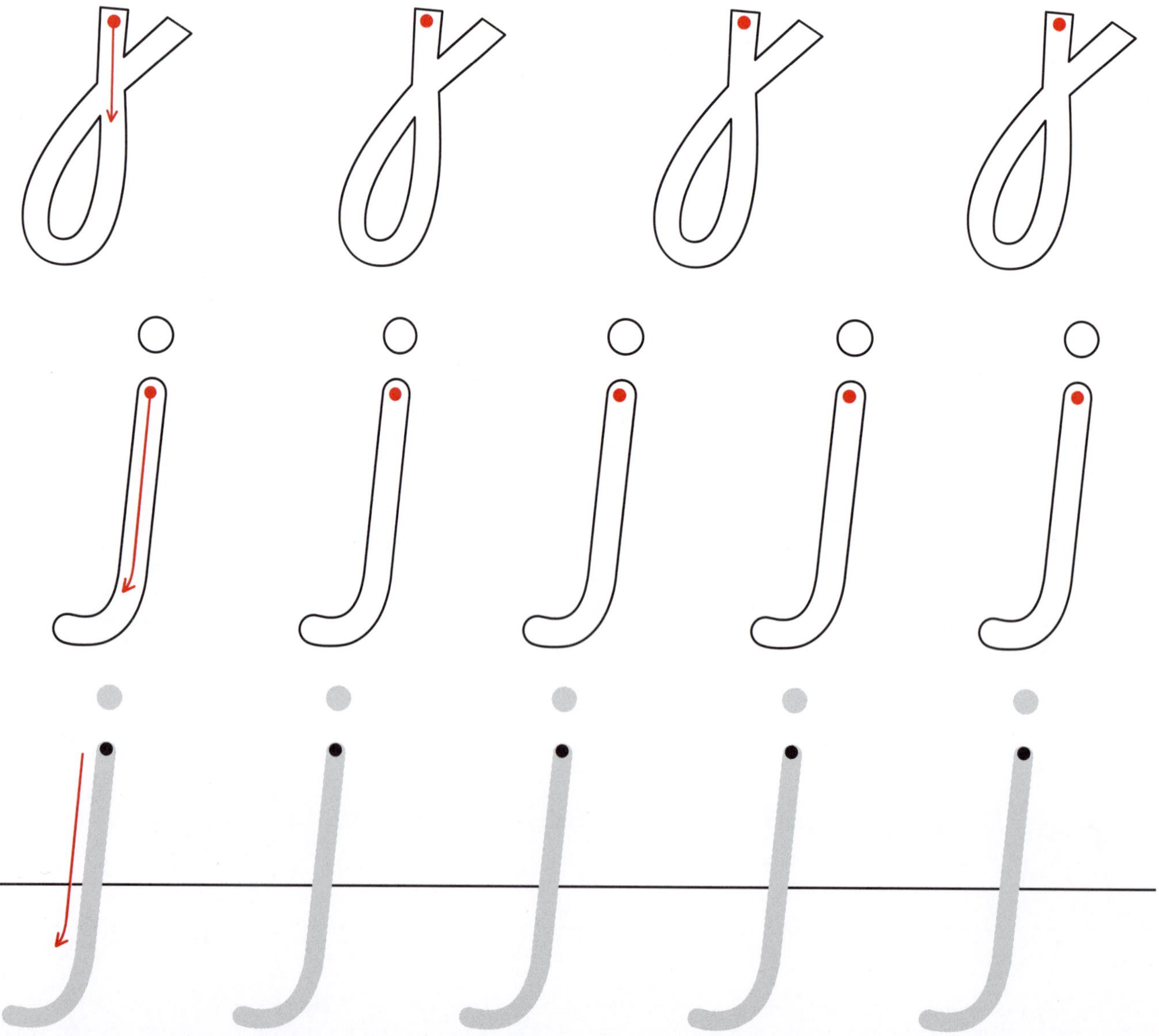

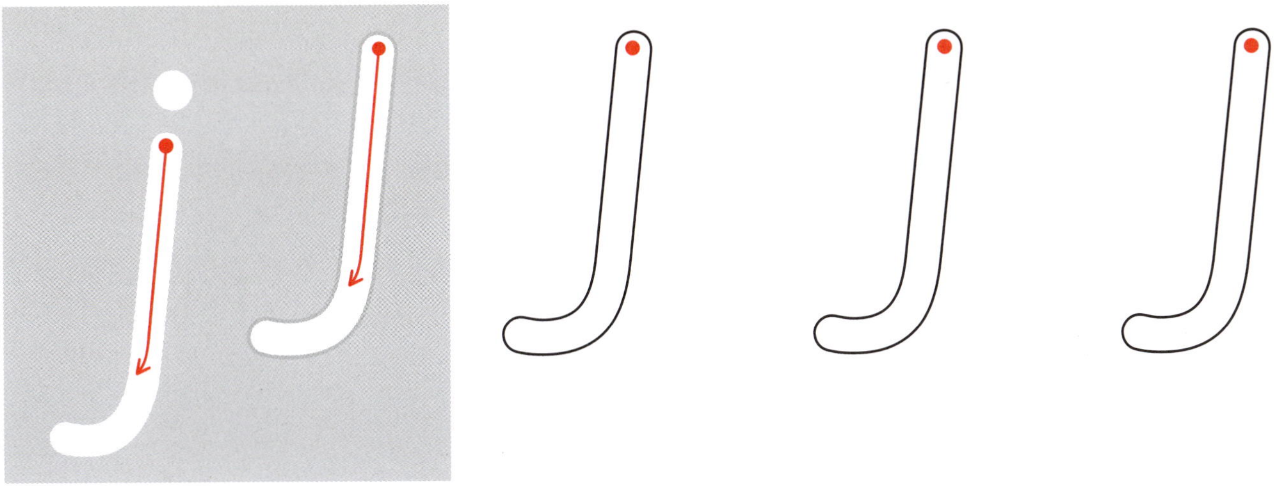

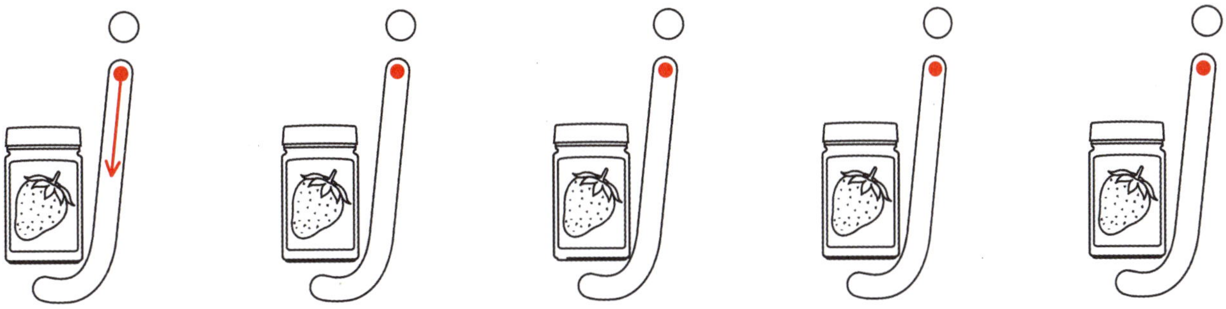

jam

jeans

Trace the letter.

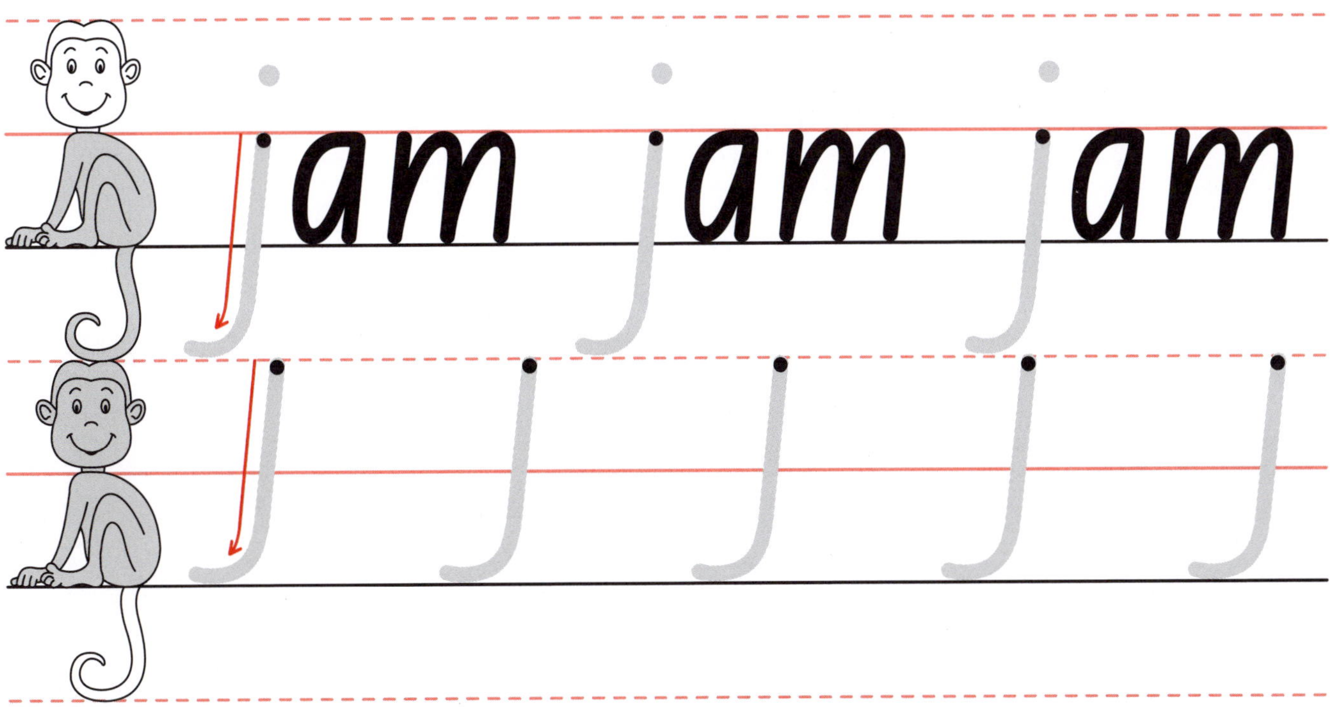

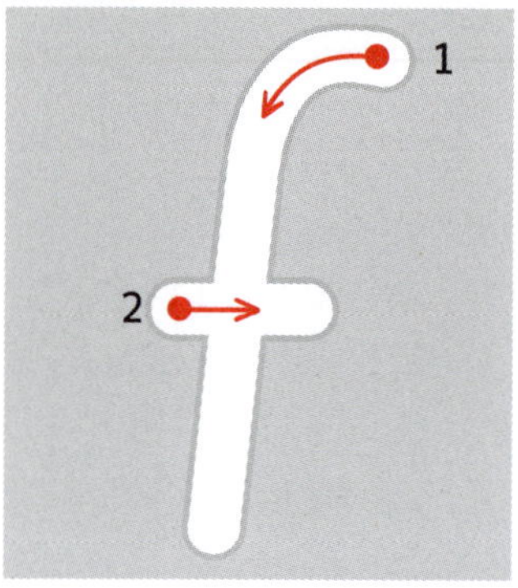

fish

Start at the dot. Follow the arrow.

feather

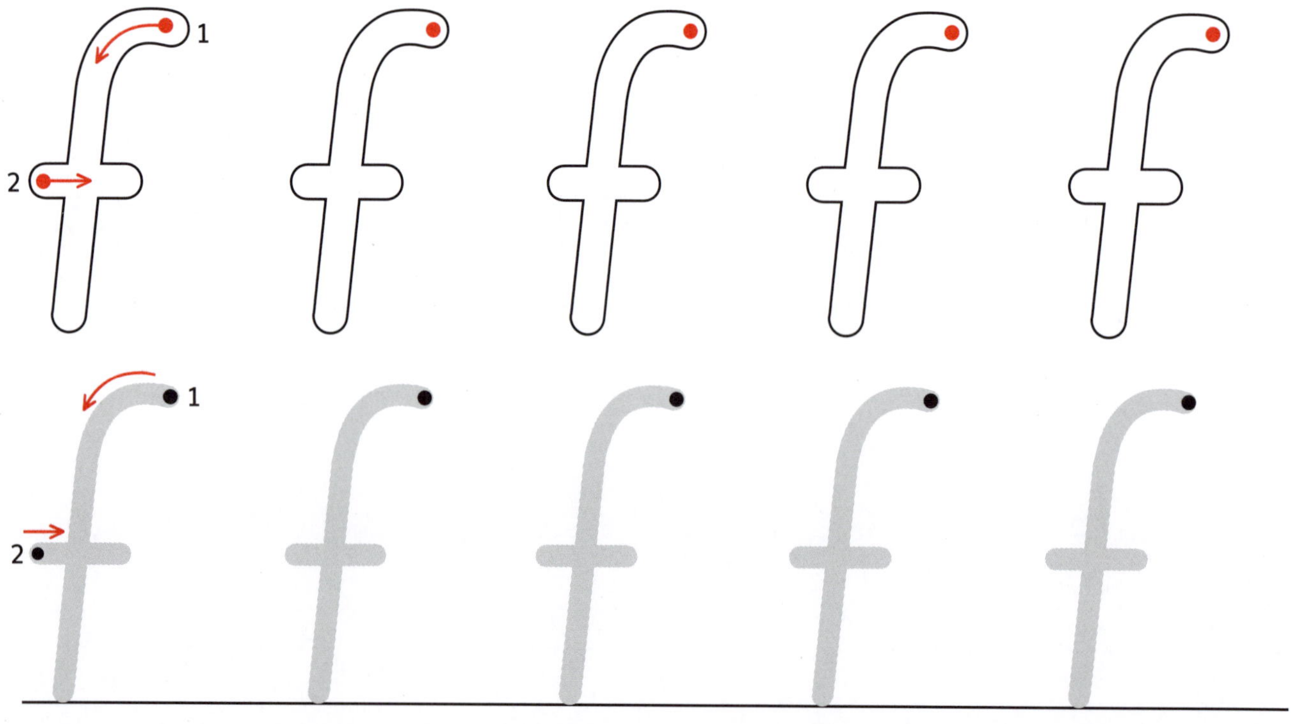

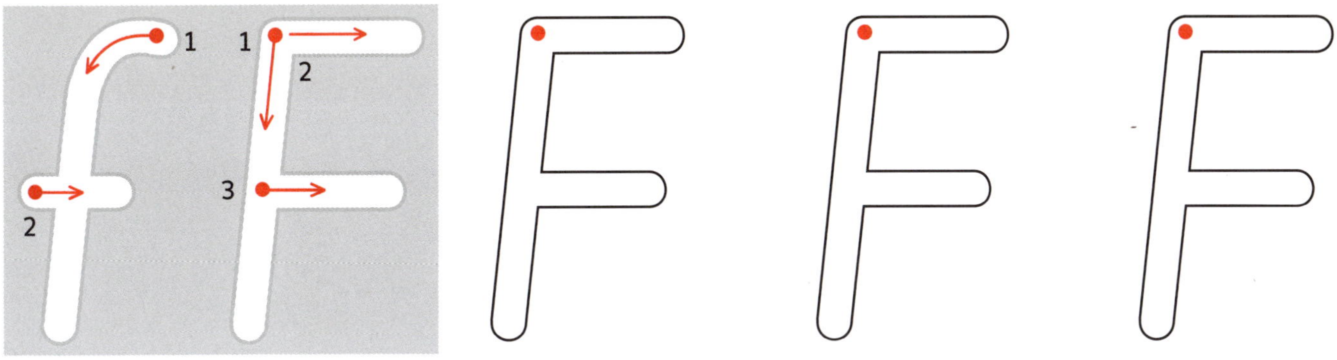

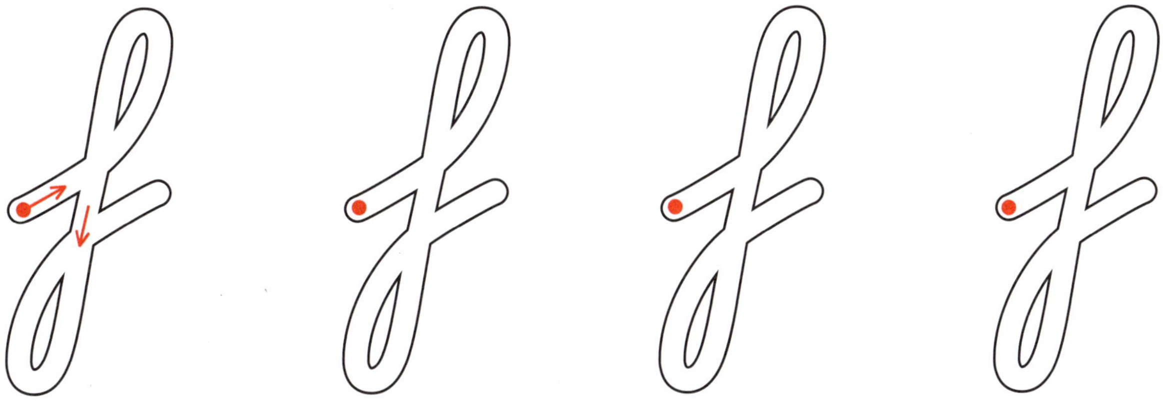

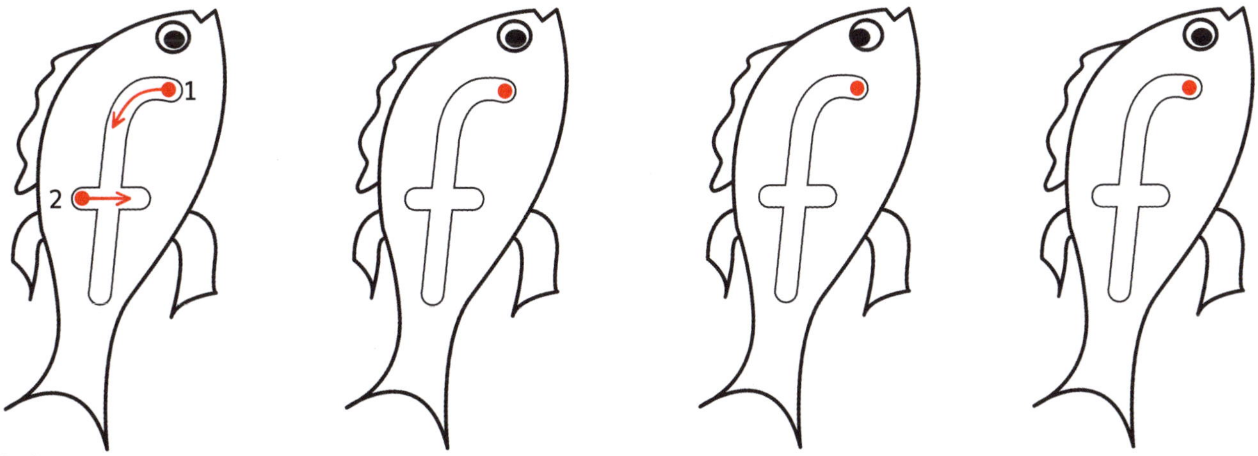

fish

Trace the letter.

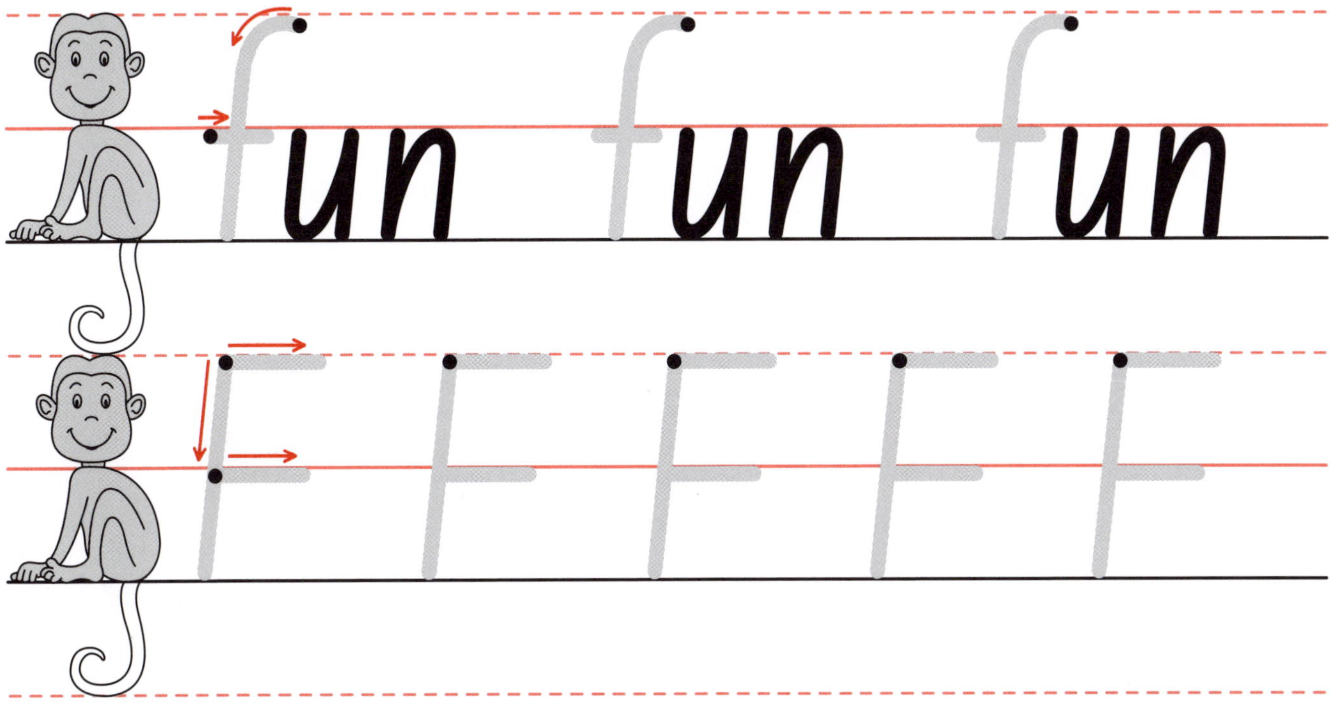

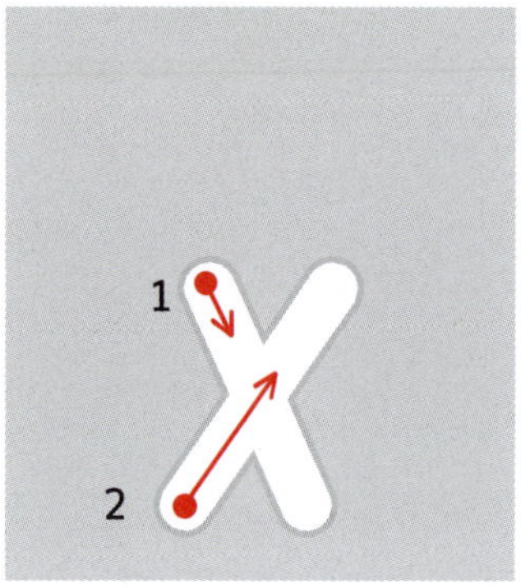

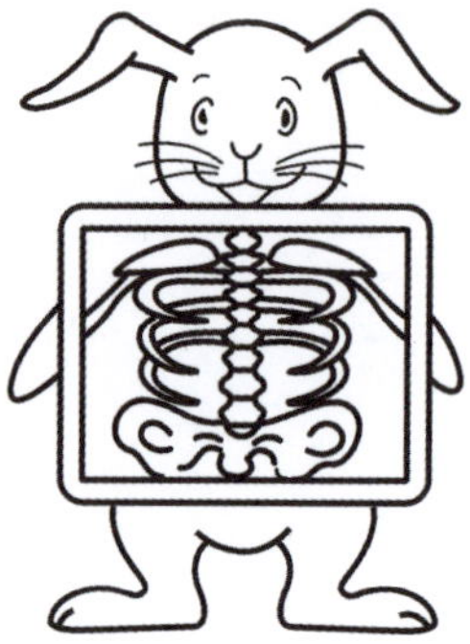

x-ray

Start at the dot. Follow the arrow.

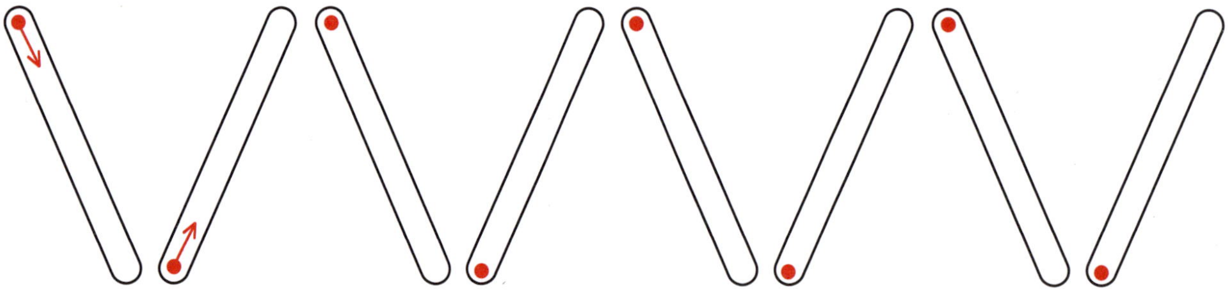

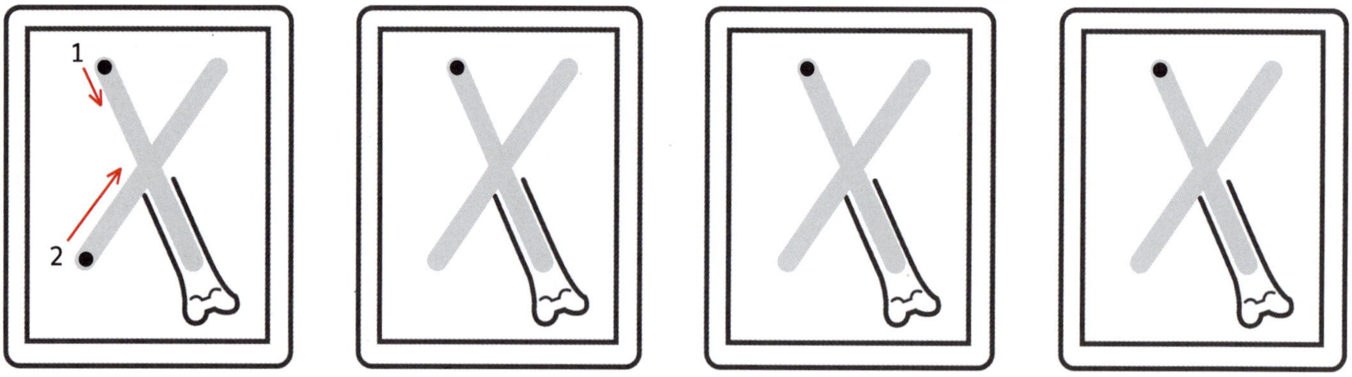

x-ray

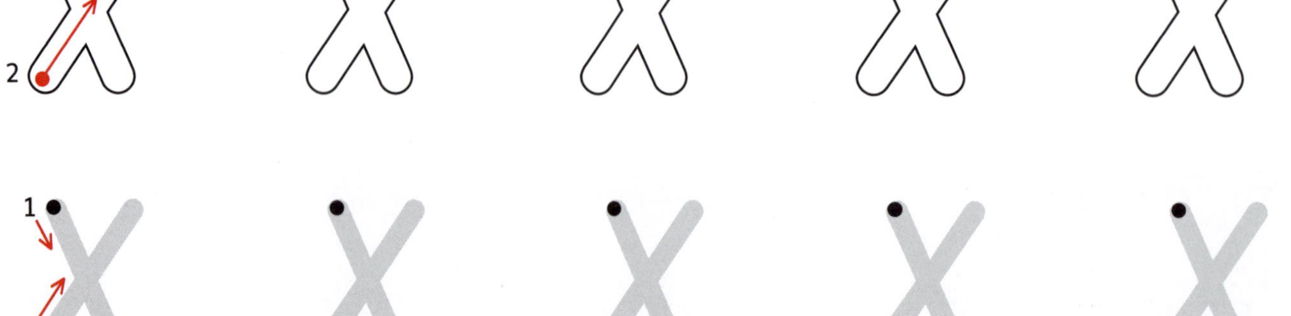

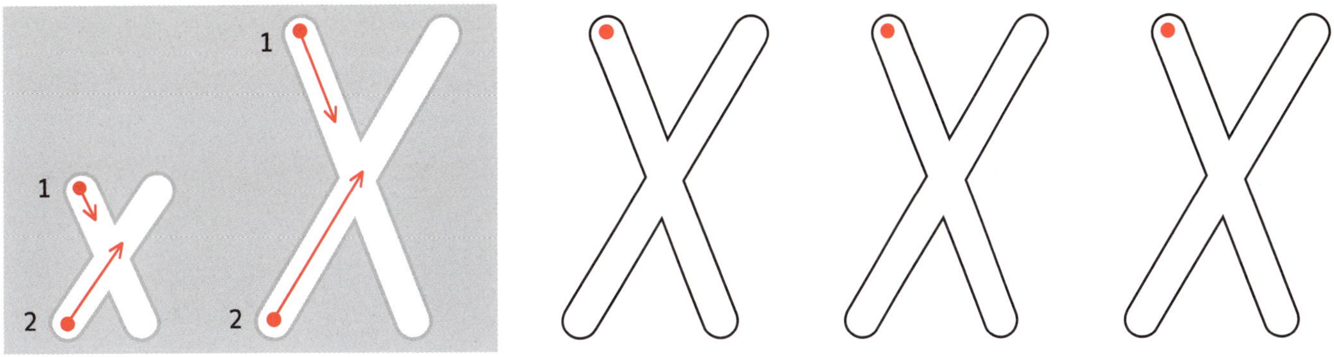

box

Trace the letter.

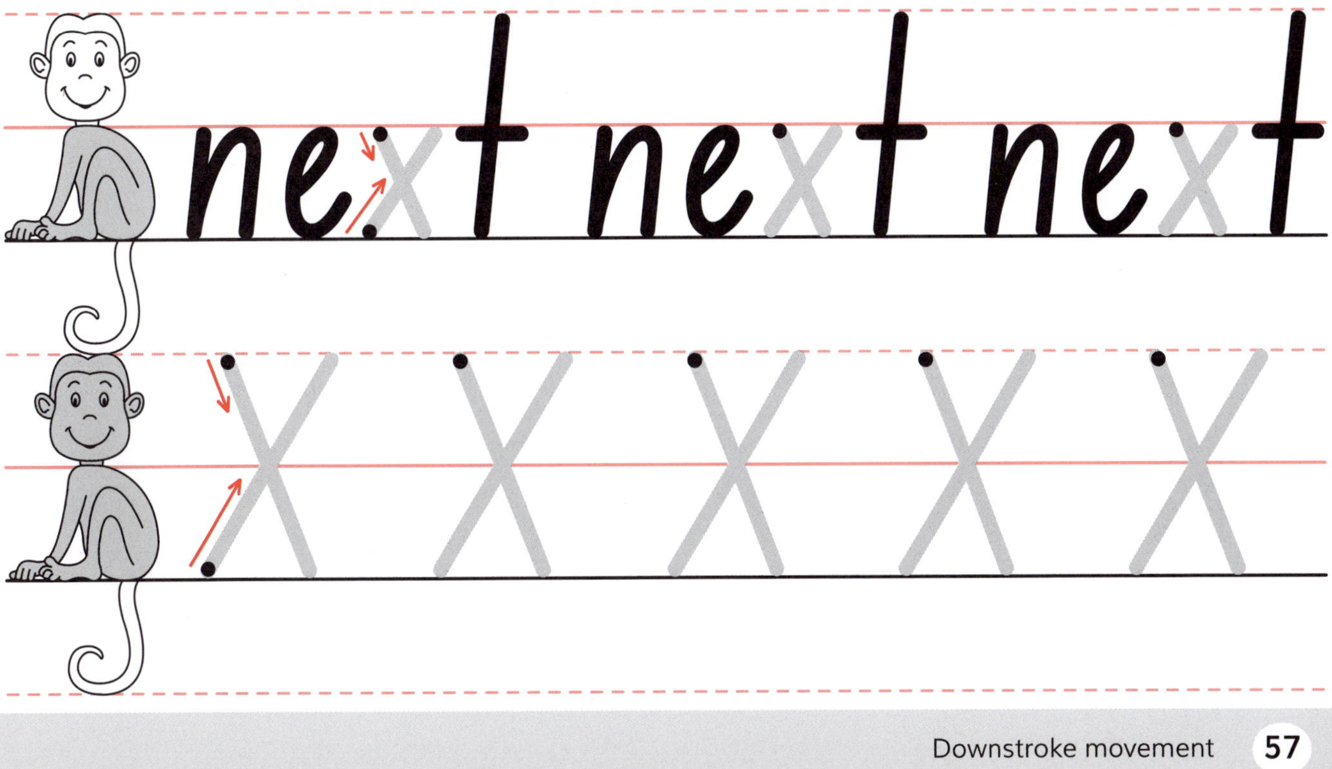

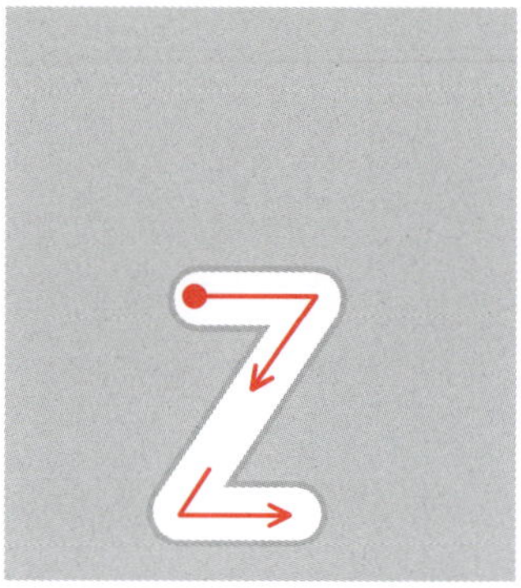

zoo

Start at the dot. Follow the arrow.

zebra

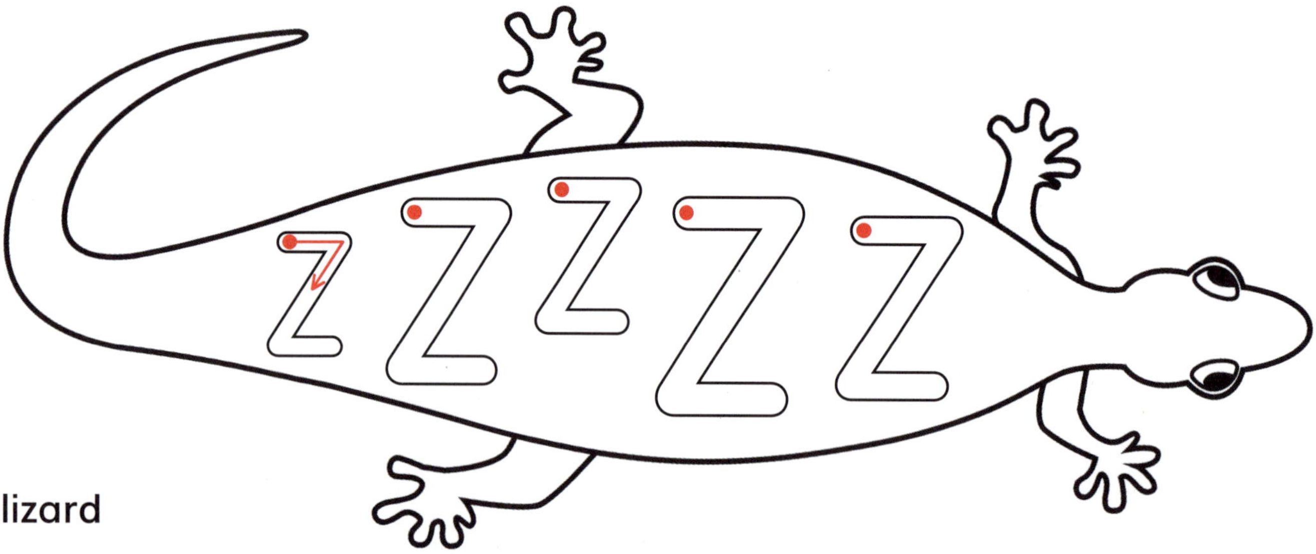

lizard

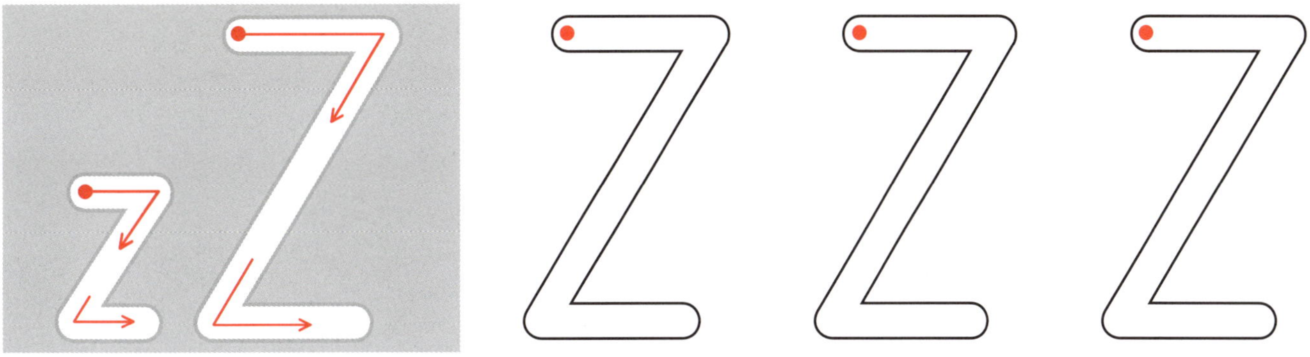

zoo

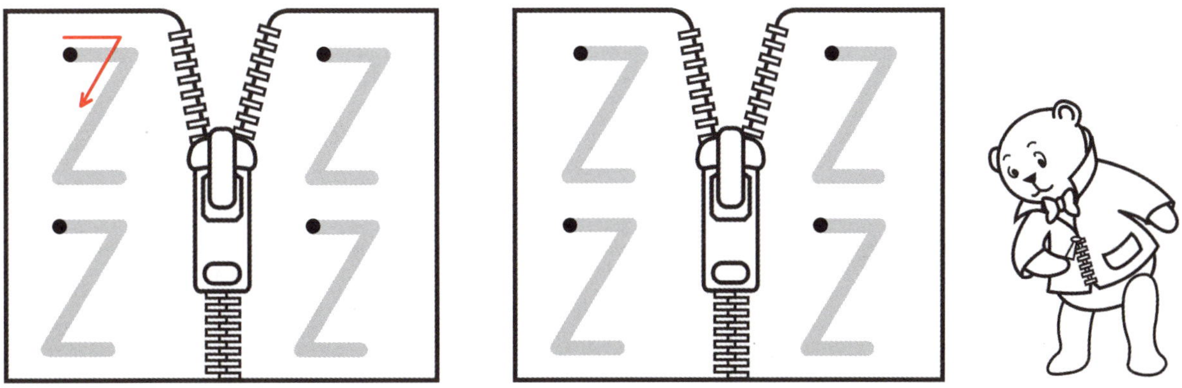

zip

Trace the letter.

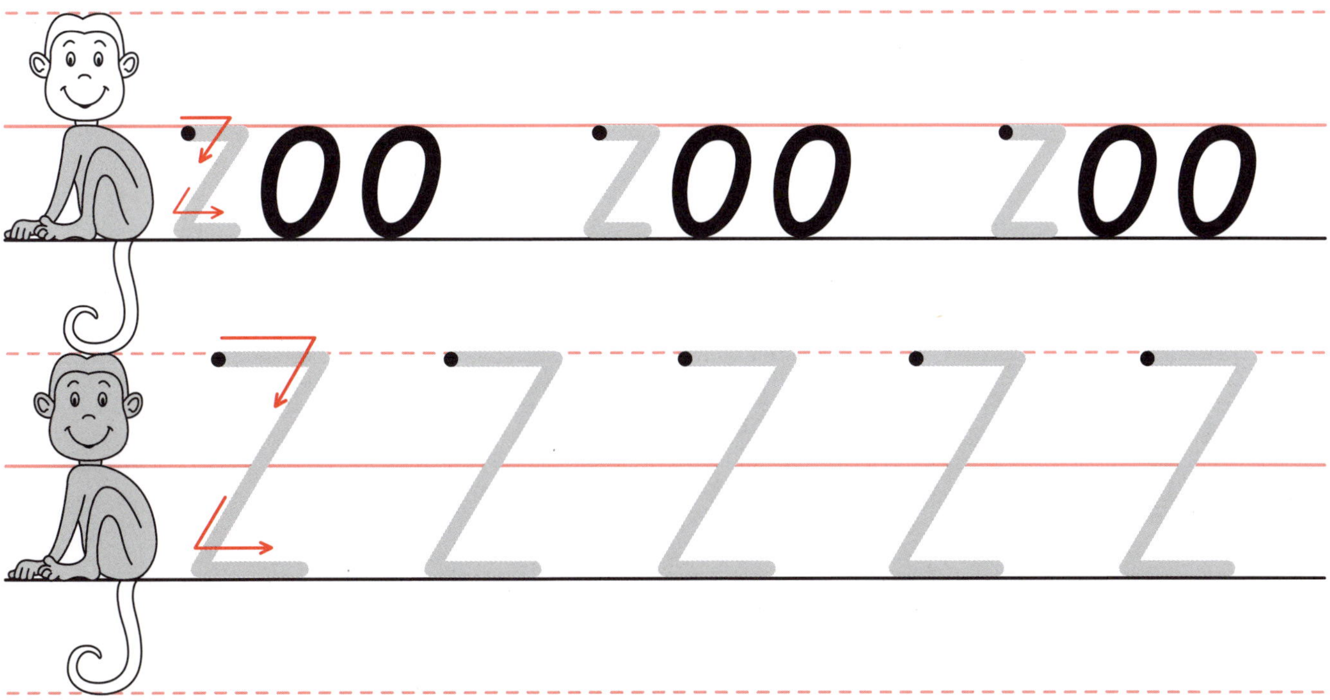

get.ga/PMWA46

Trace and copy.

1 one

2 two

3 three

Trace and copy.

1 2 4 four

1 2 5 five

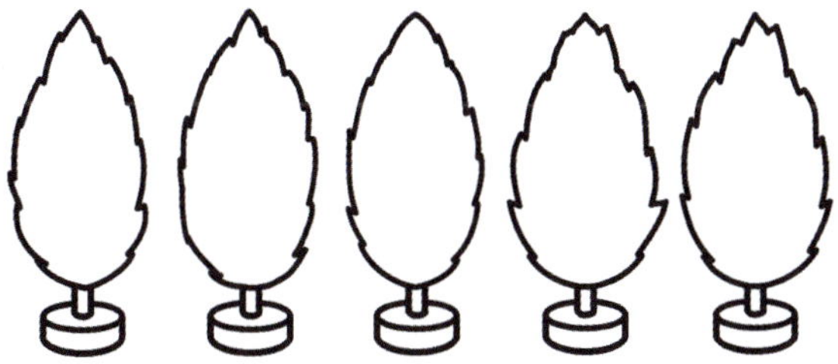

6 six

Trace and copy.

7 seven

8 eight

Trace and copy.

9 nine

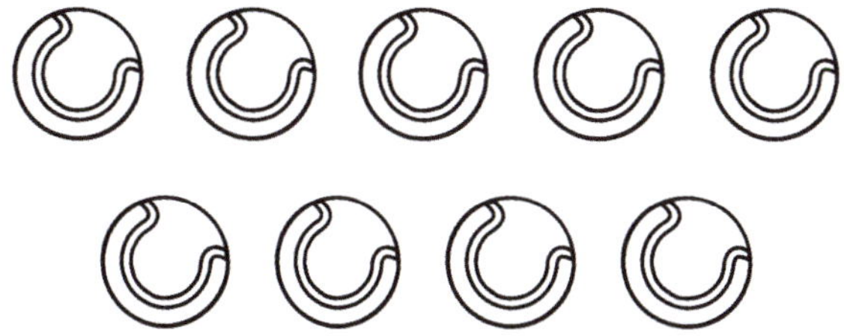

10 ten

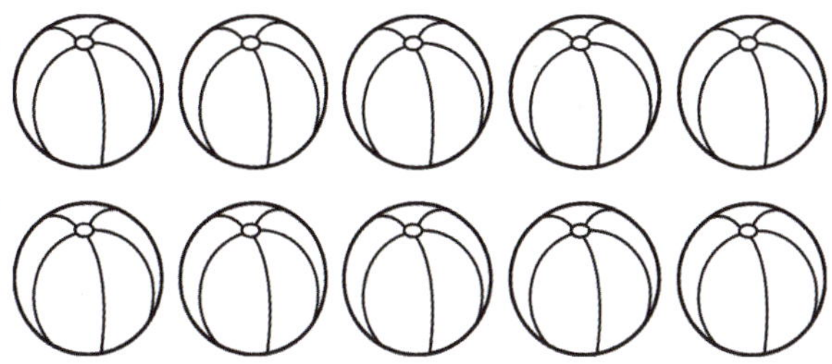

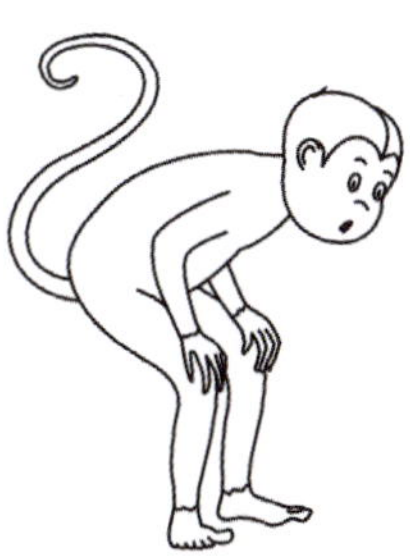

get.ga/PMWA47

Teacher observation guide

Student is: left-handed ☐ right-handed ☐

Student demonstrates correct posture, paper position and pencil grip. ☐

Student is stroking from top to bottom. ☐

Student is stroking from left to right. ☐

Student is tracking accurately using starting dots and arrows. ☐

Student is tracing accurately using starting dots and arrows. ☐

Student follows simple verbal rehearsals to form letters. ☐

Student forms lower-case letters of consistent size and with accuracy:

a	b	c	d	e	f	g	h	i	j	k	l	m	n	o	p	q	r	s	t	u	v	w	x	y	z

Student forms capital letters of consistent size and with accuracy:

A	B	C	D	E	F	G	H	I	J	K	L	M	N	O	P	Q	R	S	T	U	V	W	X	Y	Z

Student can write the numerals 1–10. ☐

Student uses head, body and tail character to describe the spatial properties of letters. ☐

Student has a growing ability to handwrite within lines. ☐

Notes:

....

....

....

....

Date: ....

CERTIFICATE

get.ga/PMWC5